First Edition

Disclaimer: The information in this book is for educational purposes only and should not be considered as professional financial, investment, or tax advice. Financial situations vary greatly among individuals, and the strategies discussed may not be suitable for everyone. Readers are encouraged to consult with qualified financial advisors, tax professionals, and other experts before making important financial decisions. The author and publisher make no representations about the accuracy or completeness of the information provided and disclaim any liability for financial losses that may result from following the advice in this book.

Rates, laws, and figures are current as of 2025 and may change. Always verify with current official sources before making financial decisions.

ISBN: 979-8-9918812-3-4

~ Discipline will set you free ~

Personal Finance for Teens and Young Adults

Smart Money Management Strategies to Build Wealth, Avoid Debt, and Achieve Financial Freedom

Table of Contents

Introduction

You're standing in line at your favorite coffee shop, phone in hand, ready to tap and pay for your usual $6 latte. As you watch the payment go through, a nagging thought crosses your mind: "Should I really be spending this much on coffee?" Maybe you've calculated that your daily coffee habit costs more than your monthly phone bill. Or perhaps you're stressing because you want to buy concert tickets for your favorite artist, but your bank account is looking pretty sad after your last shopping spree.

If this scenario sounds familiar, you're not alone. Whether you're earning money from a part-time job, receiving an allowance, or just starting to think about your financial future, you've probably experienced that uncomfortable feeling of not really understanding where your money goes or how to make it work better for you.

Here's the thing that might surprise you: that uncomfortable feeling? It's actually a superpower in disguise. The fact that you're thinking about money, questioning your spending, and wanting to understand finances better puts you light-years ahead of most people your age—and honestly, ahead of many adults too.

The Problem Nobody Talks About

Let's be real for a moment. When was the last time you had a meaningful class about money management in school? If you're like most teens and young adults, the answer is probably "never" or "barely." You might have learned about compound interest in math class or heard about the stock market in social studies, but when it comes to practical stuff—like how to build credit, choose a bank account, or save for something you actually want—school probably left you hanging.

This isn't your fault, and it's not even really your school's fault. Our education system just hasn't caught up to the reality that financial literacy is as essential as reading and writing in today's world. Meanwhile, you're expected to figure out complex financial decisions like student loans, credit cards, and investment accounts with basically zero preparation.

Add to this the fact that money conversations at home can be awkward or stressful. Maybe your family is dealing with financial challenges, making money feel scary and overwhelming. Or perhaps money has never been discussed openly, leaving you to figure things out on your own. Some of you might come from families where money isn't a daily worry, but you still feel lost about how to manage your own finances responsibly.

Then there's the social media factor. You're constantly seeing peers with the latest gadgets, clothes, and experiences, creating pressure to spend money you might not have on things you might not even want. The fear of missing out (FOMO) is real, and it can seriously mess with your financial decisions.

The statistics paint a concerning picture of financial preparedness among young people:

- In recent years, the number of states requiring a personal finance course has been growing, with nearly 30 states having such a requirement as of the mid-2020s, according to data from organizations like NGPF.org

- Only 27% of U.S. adults passed a seven-question quiz about basic financial concepts, according to a 2025 study conducted by the FINRA Foundation
- In 2025, the average American carries over $6,400 in credit card debt, a 10-year high according to TransUnion (one of the three major credit bureaus in the United States, along with Experian and Equifax)
- 59% of Americans in 2025 don't have enough savings to cover an unexpected $1,000 emergency expense
- According to the Education Data Initiative, U.S. student loan debt has reached $1.7 trillion nationally, with the average graduate owing $38,375 in federal loans

Your Secret Advantage

But here's where things get exciting. While it might feel like you're starting from behind, you actually have the most powerful wealth-building tool on your side: time.

Consider this: if you start investing just $50 a month at age 18 with a 7% annual return, you'll have over $1.3 million by the time you're 65. If you wait until you're 28 to start investing the same amount, you'll end up with about $610,000. That's literally more than double the money for starting just ten years earlier. This isn't magic—it's compound interest, and it's going to become your best friend.

Recent studies show that young people who learn basic financial principles before age 25 are 40% more likely to become millionaires during their lifetime. They're also less likely to carry credit card debt, more likely to own homes, and report higher levels of financial confidence and life satisfaction.

But the advantages of starting young go beyond just numbers. Right now, your expenses are probably relatively low. You might be living with family, on a meal plan, or just generally spending less on the big-ticket items that eat up adult budgets—like mortgages, car payments, and family expenses. This means that even small amounts of money you save and invest now can grow without you having to sacrifice your basic needs.

You're also growing up as a digital native, which gives you natural advantages in understanding and using financial technology. From mobile banking apps to investment platforms to budgeting tools, you're comfortable with technology that can make managing money easier and more intuitive than ever before.

What You'll Master

This book isn't about lecturing you on why you shouldn't buy that latte (though we will talk about mindful spending). Instead, it's about giving you the knowledge and tools to make confident financial decisions that align with your values and goals.

We'll start with **Understanding Money Basics**—not the boring stuff you might expect, but the real-world knowledge about how money actually works in your daily life. You'll learn why that $20 bill feels different from a $20 digital payment and how understanding money's role can change your relationship with it.

In **Budgeting and Expense Management**, we'll throw out the restrictive budgeting methods that make you feel deprived and instead focus on systems that help you spend money on what you actually care about while avoiding the regret purchases that drain your account.

Banking and Financial Services will demystify the world of banks, credit unions, and online financial services. You'll learn how to choose accounts that work for your lifestyle, avoid unnecessary fees, and make your money work harder for you.

Building Credit History tackles one of the most confusing aspects of adult financial life. You'll understand how to build credit responsibly, avoid common credit mistakes, and set yourself up for major purchases like cars and homes down the road.

The **Saving and Investment Basics** section will introduce you to the world of growing your money beyond traditional savings accounts. We'll cover everything from high-yield savings to index funds, making investing feel accessible rather than intimidating.

Education Financing addresses the elephant in the room for many young people: paying for college or trade school. You'll learn about different funding options, how to minimize debt, and ways to maximize the return on your education investment.

Income Generation and Career Development goes beyond just finding a job. We'll explore side hustles, freelancing, skill development, and career strategies that can boost your earning potential throughout your life.

Financial Goal Setting and Planning brings everything together, helping you create a personalized roadmap for your financial future, whether you're dreaming of traveling the world, starting a business, or achieving early retirement.

Scams, Fraud & The Money Tricks Your Brain Plays On You shows you how to avoid instances in which we might lose our hard-earned money not from bad management, but because of psychological tricks including third-party attacks that go unnoticed until it's too late.

The Transformation Ahead

By the time you finish this book, you'll have something that most adults lack: financial confidence. You'll understand how to make your money work for you instead of constantly worrying about where it went. You'll have systems in place that make good financial decisions automatic rather than stressful.

More importantly, you'll have a plan. Not just a vague idea that you should "save more money," but a clear, actionable roadmap that connects your daily money decisions to your bigger life goals. Whether you want to graduate debt-free, travel extensively, start a business, buy a home, or achieve financial independence, you'll know exactly what steps to take.

This financial confidence will ripple into other areas of your life too. When you're not stressed about money, you can focus better on school, relationships, and personal growth. When you understand how to manage money well, you'll make better decisions about everything from career choices to major purchases.

You'll also develop what financial experts call "money mindfulness"—the ability to make conscious, intentional decisions about spending and saving rather than just reacting to impulses or social pressure. This skill alone will save you thousands of dollars and countless hours of financial stress over your lifetime.

Setting Realistic Expectations

Let's be honest about something: this isn't a get-rich-quick scheme, and good financial habits don't develop overnight. Building wealth is more like getting in shape than winning the lottery—it requires consistency, patience, and gradual progress rather than dramatic overnight changes.

You won't become a millionaire by next year (unless you already are one, in which case, congratulations and you still need to know how to manage it!). You will, however, start seeing positive changes in your financial life relatively quickly. Within a month of implementing the strategies in this book, you'll likely notice less money stress and more clarity about your spending. Within a year, you could have an emergency fund, improved credit score, and a clear investment strategy.

The real magic happens over the long term. The habits you build now and the knowledge you gain will compound over the years, just like your investments. The 20-something you who understands credit scores and investment accounts will have opportunities that others don't. The 30-something you who started saving and investing early will have financial flexibility that creates more life choices.

Some of the concepts in this book might feel challenging at first, especially if you're starting with limited money or financial stress. That's completely normal and expected. We'll address different starting points throughout the book, with strategies for everyone from the teen who's never had a bank account to the young adult who's already earning a decent income. No matter where you're starting, what matters is that you *are* starting. This book will help you navigate money with confidence instead of confusion.

So take a breath. You don't have to figure everything out today. You just have to be open, curious, and willing to take the next step. One chapter at a time, you'll gain tools that can help you feel more in control of your money and your future.

Let's go build the life you actually want—on your terms, with your money, and with confidence.

Chapter 1: Understanding Money Basics

Let's go back to the line at your favorite coffee shop where you are about to buy that $6 specialty drink you've been craving all week. As you tap to pay, a thought crosses your mind –"Wait, what exactly IS money, and why does the ability to spend it has so much power over my life?"

If you've ever wondered about the magic behind money, you're asking the right questions. Understanding money isn't just about knowing how to spend it (though let's be honest, most of us have that part figured out). It's about understanding what money really is, how it works, and most importantly, how to make it work FOR you instead of against you.

Let's go through the fundamentals that'll give you the financial foundation you need to win with money – no boring economics textbook required.

Financial Literacy Fundamentals

What Money Actually Does (It's More Than You Think)

Before we talk about making money, saving money, or investing money, let's get clear on what money actually IS. Money isn't just those bills in your wallet or the numbers in your bank account – it's a tool that serves three main purposes.

Money Tip: Think of money like your smartphone – it's not valuable because it's a pretty piece of technology, but because of all the things it can DO for you.

Medium of Exchange

This is the fancy way of saying money lets you trade stuff without having to barter. Imagine if you had to trade your old gaming console directly for groceries, then trade some of those groceries for gas money. Exhausting, right? Money simplifies everything by being something everyone agrees has value. When you work at your part-time job, you're essentially trading your time and skills for money, which you can then trade for literally anything else you want.

Store of Value

Money holds its worth over time (mostly). That $20 bill you found in your winter coat from last year? It's still worth $20. This is what lets you save money today and spend it later. However – and this is important – money doesn't store value perfectly because of something called inflation, which we'll talk about in a minute.

Unit of Account

Money gives us a way to measure and compare the value of different things. How do you know if that $200 concert ticket is worth it? You compare it to other things that cost $200 – maybe 20 trips to Chipotle, or half of your monthly car payment. Money gives us a common language for talking about value.

Income vs. Wealth: The Difference That Changes Everything

Here's where a lot of people get confused, and honestly, social media doesn't help. You see influencers flashing expensive cars and designer clothes, and you assume they're wealthy. But here's the plot twist – they might just have high income, which is completely different from wealth.

Income is money flowing IN – your paycheck, your side hustle earnings, that birthday money from grandma. It's the money you earn.

Wealth is money you've accumulated and kept over time. It's your net worth – basically what you own minus what you owe.

Financial Reality: Someone making $100,000 a year who spends $105,000 is actually getting poorer every year, while someone making $40,000 who saves $5,000 is building wealth.

Think about it like this: income is like the water flowing from your faucet, and wealth is like the water you've managed to collect in buckets. You could have the strongest water flow in the world, but if you don't have any buckets (or if your buckets have holes), you'll never accumulate any water.

This is why you'll sometimes hear about professional athletes or celebrities going broke despite earning millions. High income without smart money management doesn't automatically create wealth.

Setting Financial Goals That Actually Matter

Goal-setting sounds about as exciting as watching paint dry, but stick with me here. Financial goals are basically your money GPS – without them, you're just driving around aimlessly, burning gas (and cash) with no real destination.

Let's break down goals into three categories that actually make sense for your life:

Short-term Goals (Under 1 Year)

These are your "I want this soon" goals. Maybe you want to:

Save $500 for a spring break trip

Buy a new laptop for school

Build a $1,000 emergency fund

Pay off that credit card you maybe shouldn't have gotten

Short-term goals should be specific and achievable. Instead of "save money," try "save $50 per month for 6 months to buy concert tickets."

Medium-term Goals (1-5 Years)

These are your "I'm working toward this" goals:

Save for a car down payment

Graduate college debt-free (or with minimal debt)

Move out of your parents' house

Start a small business

Take that dream trip to Europe

Medium-term goals require more planning and consistent effort, but they're not so far away that they feel impossible.

Long-term Goals (5+ Years)

These are your "future me will thank current me" goals:

Buy a house

Retire comfortably (yes, even at 18, you should be thinking about this)

Build generational wealth

Achieve financial independence

Money Tip: Write down one goal from each category and put the paper somewhere you'll see it daily. Your bathroom mirror works great – you'll be reminded every morning while brushing your teeth.

Economic Concepts That Actually Affect Your Life

I know, I know – economics sounds boring. But these concepts directly impact your money, so let's make them relevant to your actual life.

Inflation: Why Your Money Loses Buying Power

Inflation is basically when things get more expensive over time. Remember when a movie ticket cost $8? Now it's probably $12+. That's inflation in action. The opposite is deflation, when things get cheaper. Inflation is a very interesting topic yet complex. There are many books and different schools of economic thought that try to explain it.

Here's why this matters to you: if you stuff $1,000 under your mattress and inflation is 3% per year, after 10 years, that $1,000 will only buy about $740 worth of today's stuff. This is why just saving money isn't enough – you need to make your money grow faster than inflation.

Financial Reality: The average inflation rate is about 2-3% per year. While the Federal Reserve aims for a target inflation rate of around 2% per year, recent years have shown that this can fluctuate significantly, sometimes rising much higher and making it even more important to understand its impact. If your savings account earns 0.5% interest, you're actually losing money over time.

Interest Rates: Your Friend or Enemy

Interest rates determine how much it costs to borrow money and how much you earn when you save or invest. When interest rates are low:

It's cheaper to borrow money (good for loans, bad for savings)

Savings accounts pay almost nothing

People tend to spend more and save less

When interest rates are high:

Borrowing costs more (bad for loans, good for discouraging debt)

Savings accounts actually pay decent returns

People tend to save more

As a young person, pay attention to interest rates when you're considering student loans, car loans, or choosing where to keep your savings.

Supply and Demand: Why Prices Change

This one's pretty intuitive. When lots of people want something and there isn't much of it, prices go up. When there's plenty of something and not many people want it, prices go down.

Real-world example: Concert tickets for a popular artist in a small venue = high demand, low supply = expensive tickets. But streaming that same artist's music = high supply, low additional cost = cheap monthly subscription.

Understanding supply and demand helps you make smarter purchasing decisions and even spot potential investment opportunities.

Types of Income

Now let's talk about the different ways money can flow into your life. Most people think there's only one way to make money – get a job, work hard, get paid. But there are actually four main types of income, and understanding all of them is like having a complete toolkit instead of just a hammer.

Earned Income: Trading Time for Money

This is probably what you're most familiar with – you work, you get paid. Earned income includes:

Wages and salaries from your part-time job, internship, or full-time position

Tips from service jobs (shoutout to all the servers and baristas out there)

Commissions from sales positions

Bonuses for good performance

Earned income is great because it's predictable and you have a lot of control over it. Work more hours, make more money. Get promoted, make more money. Pretty straightforward.

But here's the catch: earned income has a ceiling. There are only 24 hours in a day, and you can't work all of them. Plus, the moment you stop working, the money stops coming. This is why wealthy people don't rely solely on earned income.

Money Tip: Even if you're just starting with earned income, always pay yourself first. Set up automatic transfers so a portion of every paycheck goes straight to savings before you have a chance to spend it.

Passive Income: Money That Works While You Sleep

Passive income is the holy grail of personal finance – money that comes in without you actively working for it. Now, before you get too excited, let me be clear: there's usually nothing "passive" about setting up passive income. It requires upfront work, money, or both.

Types of passive income include:

Rental Properties

Buy a property, rent it out, collect monthly rent checks. Sounds simple, but it requires significant upfront capital and ongoing management (or paying someone else to manage it).

Dividends

Some companies pay shareholders a portion of their profits. If you own stock in these companies, you get dividend payments – usually quarterly. With $10,000 invested in dividend-paying stocks averaging 3% yield, you'd earn about $300 per year without doing anything.

Interest

Money you earn from savings accounts, CDs, or bonds. Right now, high-yield savings accounts might pay 4-5% annually, which isn't bad for money just sitting there.

Royalties

If you create something – music, books, apps, YouTube videos – you can earn royalties every time someone buys or uses your creation. This is why some musicians make millions years after releasing a hit song.

Financial Reality: Building meaningful passive income usually takes years and requires either significant upfront money or a lot of initial work. Don't fall for "easy passive income" schemes – they're usually too good to be true.

Portfolio Income: Making Money from Investments

Portfolio income comes from buying and selling investments. This includes:

Capital Gains

When you buy a stock for $100 and sell it for $150, that $50 profit is a capital gain. Same concept applies to crypto, real estate, collectibles, or any other investment that increases in value.

Investment Returns

The money your investments make through a combination of growth and dividends. If you invest $1,000 in an index fund and it grows to $1,100 over the year, you've earned a 10% return.

Trading Profits

Money made from actively buying and selling investments. This is different from long-term investing – traders try to profit from short-term price movements.

Money Tip: For beginners, focus on long-term investing rather than trading. Studies show that most day traders lose money, while long-term investors who buy and hold diversified investments tend to build wealth over time.

Side Hustles: The Modern Way to Boost Income

Side hustles are the perfect way for young people to increase income while maintaining flexibility. The gig economy has created tons of opportunities that didn't exist for previous generations.

Popular side hustles include:

Freelancing

Use skills you already have – writing, graphic design, social media management, tutoring, web development. Platforms like Upwork, Fiverr, and Freelancer make it easy to find clients.

Gig Economy Jobs

Rideshare driving (Uber, Lyft)
Food delivery (DoorDash, Uber Eats, Grubhub)
Task services (TaskRabbit, Handy)
Pet services (Rover, Wag)

Small Business Ventures

Dropshipping
Print-on-demand products
Local services (lawn care, house cleaning, pet sitting)
Selling handmade items on Etsy

Online Sales

Flipping items from thrift stores or garage sales
Selling your own stuff you no longer need

Amazon FBA (Fulfillment by Amazon)
Creating and selling digital products

Money Tip: Choose a side hustle that either pays well per hour or teaches you valuable skills (or both). Delivering food might pay your bills, but learning graphic design could become a full-time career.

The beauty of side hustles is that they can eventually grow into passive or portfolio income. That freelance writing gig could become a content agency. That Etsy shop could become a full-blown e-commerce business.

Financial Institutions

Let's talk about where to actually keep your money and how different financial institutions can help (or hurt) your financial goals. Not all banks are created equal, and choosing the right ones can literally save you thousands of dollars over your lifetime.

Traditional Banks: The Old School Option

Traditional banks are the big names you see everywhere – Chase, Bank of America, Wells Fargo, etc. They offer the full suite of services:

Checking Accounts

Your day-to-day money account. You deposit paychecks here, pay bills from here, and use your debit card to access this money. Most checking accounts pay little to no interest, but they offer convenience and easy access to your money.

Savings Accounts

Where you keep money you don't need immediate access to. Traditional bank savings accounts typically pay very low interest rates – often less than 1% annually. They're safe and FDIC insured (meaning the government protects your money up to $250,000), but they won't help you build wealth.

Loans

Banks offer various types of loans – personal loans, auto loans, mortgages, and student loans. The interest rates and terms vary widely, so it's always worth shopping around.

Safety Deposit Boxes

Secure storage for important documents and valuables. Useful for things like birth certificates, passports, and expensive jewelry, but not necessary for most young people.

Financial Reality: Traditional banks make money by paying you very little interest on your deposits and charging much higher interest on loans. That's their business model, and there's nothing wrong with it – just be aware of it.

Credit Unions: The Community Alternative

Credit unions are like banks, but they're owned by their members (customers) rather than shareholders. This structure often leads to:

Lower fees on accounts and services

Better interest rates on both savings and loans

More personalized service since they're usually smaller and community-focused

Easier loan approval since they're more willing to look at your whole financial picture, not just your credit score

The downside? Credit unions often have fewer locations and ATMs, and their technology (apps, websites) might not be as advanced as big banks.

Money Tip: If there's a credit union you can join (through school, work, or community membership), it's often worth comparing their rates and fees to traditional banks.

Online Banks: The Digital-First Option

Online banks have become incredibly popular, especially among young people who do most of their banking through apps anyway. They typically offer:

Higher Interest Rates

Since online banks don't have to pay for physical branches, they can pass those savings on to customers. High-yield savings accounts from online banks might pay 4-5% annually compared to 0.5% from traditional banks.

Lower Fees

Many online banks have no monthly maintenance fees, no minimum balance requirements, and reimburse ATM fees since they don't have their own ATM networks.

Better Technology

Online banks usually have superior mobile apps and websites since that's their primary way of serving customers.

Popular online banks include Ally Bank, Marcus by Goldman Sachs, Capital One 360, and Discover Bank.

The main downside is no physical locations, so you can't walk in and talk to someone face-to-face. But honestly, when's the last time you went inside a bank branch?

Money Tip: Consider keeping your checking account at a traditional bank or credit union for convenience, but moving your savings to a high-yield online savings account to earn more interest.

Investment Firms: Planning for the Future

Investment firms help you grow your money over time through various investment products:

Brokerage Accounts

These let you buy and sell stocks, bonds, ETFs, and other investments. Many firms now offer commission-free stock trading, making it easier than ever to start investing with small amounts.

Popular options for beginners include:

Fidelity and **Charles Schwab** (traditional firms with great apps)

Robinhood (simple, mobile-first platform)

E*TRADE (good educational resources)

Merrill Edge (easy integration with Bank of America)

Robo-Advisors

These are automated investment platforms that create and manage a diversified portfolio for you based on your goals and risk tolerance. Examples include Betterment, Wealthfront, and robo-advisor services from traditional firms.

Financial Advisors

Human professionals who provide personalized financial advice. Most young people don't need a financial advisor yet, but they can be valuable once you have more complex financial situations or significant assets.

Retirement Accounts

Investment firms can help you set up IRAs (Individual Retirement Accounts) to start saving for retirement. Yes, even if you're 18, you should be thinking about retirement. Why? Because starting early gives your money more time to grow through the power of compound interest. Even small contributions in your teens and twenties can snowball into serious wealth by the time you're older.

Chapter 2: Budgeting and Expense Management

You just got your first real paycheck, and you're staring at that direct deposit notification feeling like you've won the lottery. Finally, some actual money to call your own! But then reality hits – rent is due, your car needs gas, you promised your friend you'd go to that concert, and somehow you also need to eat actual food. Suddenly, that paycheck doesn't seem quite as massive as it did five minutes ago.

If this sounds familiar, welcome to the club! Managing money when you're starting out can feel like trying to solve a puzzle where half the pieces are missing. The good news? Budgeting isn't some mysterious adult skill that requires a finance degree – it's basically just a plan for your money so you can stop wondering where it all went.

Creating Your First Budget

Let's start with the truth: budgeting gets a bad rap because people think it means never having fun again. That's like saying meal planning means you can never eat pizza. Not true! A budget is actually your ticket to MORE freedom because you'll know exactly how much you can spend on the things you love without stressing about money later.

Income Assessment: Know What You're Working With

Before you can make a plan for your money, you need to know how much money you actually have coming in. This might seem obvious, but you'd be surprised how many people skip this step and wonder why their budget never works.

Job Income

If you have a part-time job, this is probably your biggest source of income. But here's the thing – always budget based on your **take-home pay**, not your gross pay. That first paycheck can be a real shock when you see how much gets taken out for taxes, Social Security, and other deductions.

Money Tip: If your hours vary from week to week, base your budget on your lowest typical month. It's way better to have extra money than to come up short because you budgeted for that one amazing week when you worked 35 hours.

Allowance and Family Support

Maybe your parents give you money for certain expenses, or you get a regular allowance. Count it, but also have a conversation about what's expected to continue and what might change. If your allowance is supposed to cover school lunches and gas money, make sure you know that upfront.

Gifts and Irregular Income

Birthday money, holiday cash, and those random times your grandma slips you a twenty – these are nice bonuses, but don't build your regular budget around them. Think of surprise money as extra funds for your savings goals or fun purchases.

Side Hustle Earnings

Babysitting, dog walking, selling stuff online, tutoring – the gig economy is perfect for young people who want flexible income. Just remember that this income can be unpredictable, so it's smart to save some of it for months when work is slower.

Financial Reality: Your income will probably change a lot in the next few years as you finish school, start new jobs, or change your living situation. That's totally normal – just update your budget when things change.

Expense Tracking: Where Does Your Money Actually Go?

Now comes the detective work. For at least a week (ideally a month), track every single dollar you spend. Yes, even that $1.50 for a candy bar. This isn't about judging your choices – it's about getting real data so you can make informed decisions.

Fixed Costs

These are expenses that stay pretty much the same every month:

Phone bill

Car insurance

Gym membership

Streaming services

Any loan payments

Fixed costs are actually the easiest to budget for because you know exactly what's coming.

Variable Costs

These change from month to month but are still regular expenses:

Gas for your car

Groceries and eating out

Entertainment

Clothing

Personal care items

Variable costs are where you have the most control over your spending, which means they're also where you can make the biggest impact on your budget.

One-Time Purchases

These are the expenses that pop up occasionally:

Car repairs

New phone

Gifts for friends and family

School supplies

Medical expenses

Money Tip: Even though these are "one-time" expenses, they happen to everyone regularly. Smart budgeters set aside a little money each month for these surprise costs.

Budget Categories: Organizing Your Money

Think of budget categories like folders on your computer – they help you organize everything so you can find what you need. Here are the main categories most young people need to think about:

Housing

If you're living at home, this might be zero, or your parents might ask you to contribute to household expenses. If you're in college or living on your own, this includes rent, utilities, and basic household supplies.

Transportation

Car payment, insurance, gas, maintenance, parking, or public transportation costs. If you don't have a car yet but are saving for one, create this category anyway and start putting money aside.

Food

Groceries, school lunch, coffee runs, and eating out with friends. Food costs can vary wildly depending on your choices, so this is a great category to focus on if you need to cut expenses.

Entertainment and Social

Movies, concerts, games, apps, hobbies, and hanging out with friends. Don't skip this category thinking you'll just "not spend money on fun" – that never works. Instead, decide how much you can afford for entertainment and stick to it.

Savings

Pay yourself first! Even if it's just $25 a month, make savings a non-negotiable part of your budget. Future you will be incredibly grateful.

Personal Care

Haircuts, skincare, makeup, clothes – the stuff that helps you feel confident and put-together.

Budget Methods: Finding Your Style

Just like there's no one-size-fits-all approach to studying or working out, there's no single budgeting method that works for everyone. Here are three popular approaches to try:

The 50/30/20 Rule

This is probably the most famous budgeting rule, and it's perfect for beginners:

50% for needs (housing, transportation, basic food, minimum debt payments)

30% for wants (entertainment, dining out, hobbies, non-essential shopping)

20% for savings and extra debt payments

Let's say you bring home $800 a month from your part-time job:

$400 for needs

$240 for wants

$160 for savings

Zero-Based Budgeting

With this method, you give every dollar a job before you spend it. Your income minus all your planned expenses should equal zero. This doesn't mean you spend everything – it means you've allocated everything, including money for savings.

Here's how it works: If you have $800 coming in, you assign all $800 to different categories. Maybe $200 for car expenses, $150 for food, $100 for entertainment, $200 for savings, and $150 for miscellaneous expenses. The key is that every dollar has a purpose.

The Envelope Method

This is old-school but incredibly effective, especially if you tend to overspend on your debit card. You put cash in different envelopes for different categories. When the envelope is empty, you're done spending in that category for the month.

You can do this digitally too – many banking apps let you create different "buckets" or savings goals that work like virtual envelopes.

Financial Reality: You probably won't nail your budget on the first try, and that's completely normal. Most people need 3-4 months to create a budget that actually works for their lifestyle.

Tracking Expenses

Creating a budget is step one, but tracking your expenses is what makes the magic happen. This is where you'll discover your money patterns and figure out why your budget isn't working (if it isn't).

Manual Tracking: Going Old School

Don't underestimate the power of simple tracking methods. Sometimes the best system is the one you'll actually use consistently.

Notebooks and Journals

Keep a small notebook with you and write down every purchase as you make it. This might seem tedious, but there's something powerful about physically writing down "$4.50 - coffee" that makes you more aware of your spending patterns.

Spreadsheets

If you're comfortable with Excel or Google Sheets, this can be a super flexible way to track expenses. You can create categories, use formulas to calculate totals, and even make charts to visualize your spending patterns.

Money Tip: Google Sheets is free and you can access it from your phone, which makes it easy to update on the go.

Receipt Collection

Get in the habit of keeping every receipt for a week, then sit down and categorize them. This is a great reality check – you might think you only spend $20 a week on coffee, but those receipts don't lie.

Apps and Tools: Let Technology Help

The best expense tracking app is the one you'll actually use. Here are some popular options that work well for young people:

YNAB (You Need A Budget)

YNAB is based on zero-based budgeting and is incredibly popular with people who are serious about getting their money under control. It costs money (around $14/month), but they offer a free trial and often have student discounts.

PocketGuard

This app is perfect if you tend to overspend. It shows you how much you have available to spend after accounting for bills, goals, and necessities. The "In My Pocket" feature literally tells you how much you can spend right now without messing up your budget.

> **Money Tip:** Most banks also have their own budgeting tools built into their apps. Check out what your bank offers before paying for a separate service.

Bank Statements: Your Financial Report Card

Your monthly bank statement is like a report card for your spending habits. Don't just glance at the balance – actually read through your transactions.

Monthly Reviews

Set aside 30 minutes each month to review your bank statement. Look for:

Subscriptions you forgot about

Fees you might be able to avoid

Spending patterns you didn't realize you had

Transactions you don't recognize (fraud happens!)

Category Analysis

Most banking apps will automatically categorize your spending. Take a look at these categories and see if any surprises jump out. You might discover you're spending way more on food delivery than you realized, or that your "small" purchases are adding up to something significant.

Spending Patterns

Do you spend more on weekends? At the beginning or end of the month? When you're stressed about school? Understanding your patterns helps you plan for them instead of being surprised by them.

Cash Flow Analysis: Timing Matters

Cash flow is just a fancy term for understanding when money comes in versus when it goes out. This is super important if you get paid irregularly or have big expenses that don't line up with your paychecks.

Money In vs Money Out

Create a simple calendar that shows when you get paid and when your major bills are due. This helps you avoid the stress of having a big expense due right before payday when your account is running low.

Timing of Payments

If possible, try to align your bill due dates with your pay schedule. Many companies will let you change your due date if you call and ask. Having all your bills due a few days after you get paid can make budgeting much simpler.

Financial Reality: Even people who are great with money have months where unexpected expenses throw off their budget. The goal isn't perfection – it's progress and awareness.

Cost-Cutting Strategies

Now for the fun part – finding ways to keep more money in your pocket without feeling like you're living on rice and beans. Smart cost-cutting isn't about being cheap; it's about being intentional with your money so you can spend on the things that really matter to you.

Student Discounts: Your Secret Weapon

Being a student has its perks, and one of the biggest ones is access to discounts that can save you serious money.

Education Pricing

Software companies love students. You can get:

Microsoft Office for free through many schools

Adobe Creative Suite for $20/month instead of $50+

Spotify Premium for $5/month instead of $10

Amazon Prime for $7/month instead of $15

Money Tip: *Always check if there's a student version before paying full price for any software or subscription service.*

Student ID Benefits

Your student ID is like a magic discount card. Flash it at:

Movie theaters (often $2-5 off tickets)

Museums and attractions

Public transportation

Some restaurants and retail stores

Sporting events and concerts

Campus Resources

Your school fees probably include access to tons of free stuff:

Gym and fitness classes

Library resources (including free movie rentals at many schools)

Career counseling and resume help

Mental health services

Sometimes even free food at events

Generic Brands: Quality Without the Premium

Store brands and generic products can save you 20-40% without sacrificing quality. The key is knowing where it matters and where it doesn't.

Store Brands That Are Usually Great
Basic medications (ibuprofen, allergy meds)

Cleaning supplies

Basic food staples (pasta, rice, canned goods)

School and office supplies

Basic clothing items (t-shirts, socks, underwear)

Where Brand Might Matter More
Electronics (though even here, research the specs, not just the brand)

Skincare products (if you have sensitive skin)

Shoes you'll wear frequently

Items you use daily and care about the experience

Money Tip: Try the store brand version of things you buy regularly. If you don't notice a difference, you've found an easy way to save money every month.

Free Alternatives: Getting Creative

Before you pay for something, ask yourself: "Is there a free version of this that would work just as well?"

Free Apps and Services

Instead of paying for photo editing: Use free apps like VSCO or Canva

Instead of paying for music: Use Spotify's free tier with ads

Instead of paying for workout classes: YouTube has thousands of free workout videos

Instead of paying for language learning: Try Duolingo before upgrading to paid apps

Library Resources

Modern libraries are incredible and way more than just books:

Free WiFi and computer access

Movie and video game rentals

Study spaces

Free classes and workshops

Sometimes even tools and equipment you can borrow

Community Events

Check your city's website, local Facebook groups, and community centers for free events:

Outdoor movie screenings

Festivals and fairs

Free museum days

Community classes

Volunteer opportunities (great for your resume too!)

Bulk Buying: When Bigger Really Is Better

Bulk buying can save you money, but only if you do it smart. The key is focusing on non-perishable items you actually use regularly.

What to Buy in Bulk

Toiletries (shampoo, toothpaste, deodorant)

Cleaning supplies

Non-perishable food (pasta, rice, canned goods)

School supplies at back-to-school sales

Items you use consistently

Bulk Buying Strategies

Split with friends or family: You don't need 24 rolls of toilet paper by yourself, but splitting a Costco pack with roommates makes sense

Calculate the per-unit cost: Sometimes the bigger size isn't actually cheaper

Only buy what you have space to store: A great deal isn't great if you don't have room for it

Focus on items with long shelf lives: Bulk buying fresh food usually leads to waste

Financial Reality: Warehouse stores like Costco and Sam's Club charge membership fees. Do the math to make sure your savings will cover the membership cost before signing up.

Smart Spending Habits

This is where budgeting gets real. Anyone can create a budget on paper, but developing smart spending habits is what actually keeps money in your account. These habits will serve you well whether you're managing $100 or $100,000.

Needs vs Wants: The Foundation of Smart Spending

This sounds simple, but in practice, it can be tricky. We're really good at convincing ourselves that wants are actually needs.

True Needs

Food (but maybe not the $15 smoothie)

Shelter

Transportation to work/school

Basic clothing

Healthcare

Minimum debt payments

Wants Disguised as Needs

"I need this specific brand of jeans" (you need pants, but any decent pants will do)

"I need to eat out because I don't have time to cook" (you need food, but you have options)

"I need the latest iPhone because my current one is slow" (you need a working phone)

The Priority Ranking System

When you want to buy something, rate it on a scale of 1-10:

9-10: Things that significantly improve your life or help you reach important goals.

6–8: Nice-to-haves that add value or fun but aren't critical.

1–5: Impulse buys or short-term thrills that don't align with your goals (like another random phone accessory or fast food just because you're bored).

This kind of mental ranking helps you slow down and spend with intention. And the cool part? Over time, it becomes a habit.

Remember: budgeting isn't about cutting out all joy—it's about making space for what matters most. When you're in control of your money, you're also in control of your time, energy, and future options. And that's a great feeling!

The 10-10-10 Rule

When you're tempted to make a purchase, ask yourself: How will I feel about this in 10 minutes, 10 months, and 10 years? That $200 sneaker drop might feel amazing for 10 minutes, okay for 10 months, but in 10 years? You probably won't even remember them.

Once you start thinking this way, you'll notice your spending habits shift. You'll make more intentional choices, feel less guilt about the things you *do* spend on, and save way more without feeling like you're sacrificing.

Remember, budgeting isn't about being perfect or depriving yourself. It's about knowing your money, owning your decisions, and building the life you want—one smart choice at a time.

Next up, we'll take a deeper look at the financial tools and services that can support your journey. You've built the plan. Now let's build the system.

Chapter 3: Banking and Financial Services

You just got your first real job, and your boss mentions setting up direct deposit. Suddenly you realize you need an actual bank account – not just the savings account your parents opened when you were eight with your birthday money still sitting there. Or maybe you're tired of asking your parents to Venmo you money, then having them transfer it from their account. Either way, welcome to one of your first major adult financial decisions!

Here's the thing about banking – it's not just about having a place to stash your cash. Your bank becomes your financial home base, and choosing the right one can literally save you hundreds of dollars a year (or cost you that much if you pick wrong). The good news? You don't need to be intimidated by all the options. Let's break this down so you can walk into any bank or browse any banking website like you know exactly what you're doing.

Choosing Your First Bank Account

Account Types: Finding Your Financial Match

Think of bank accounts like dating – you want to find the one that fits your lifestyle and treats you right. Let's talk about your options:

Checking Accounts: Your Financial Daily Driver

Your checking account is like your wallet's best friend. This is where your paycheck lands, where you pay bills from, and what connects to your debit card. It's designed for money that moves – in and out, constantly.

Most checking accounts don't pay much interest (we're talking maybe 0.01% – basically nothing), but that's okay because this isn't where you're trying to grow money. This is your spending money headquarters.

Money Tip: Look for checking accounts with no minimum balance requirements when you're starting out. Some banks offer student accounts with even better perks if you're in high school or college.

Savings Accounts: Your Goal-Getting Partner

Your savings account is where you stash money for specific goals or emergencies. Unlike checking, you typically can't spend directly from savings (no debit card), which is actually a good thing – it creates a mental barrier that helps you not accidentally spend your emergency fund on late-night food delivery.

Savings accounts usually pay higher interest than checking, though we're still not talking about getting rich off the interest. The real power is in building the habit of saving consistently.

Money Market Accounts: The Hybrid Option

Money market accounts are like the cool older sibling of savings accounts. They typically pay higher interest than regular savings but require higher minimum balances. Some let you write a few checks per month or have limited debit card access.

Financial Reality: Unless you're starting with at least $1,000-$2,500, money market accounts probably aren't your first choice. Focus on getting a solid checking and savings combo first.

Fee Structures: Don't Let Banks Nickel and Dime You

Here's where banks can either be your friend or become that expensive habit you didn't see coming. Let's talk about the fees that can absolutely wreck your budget if you're not careful:

Monthly Maintenance Fees: The Subscription You Don't Want

Some banks charge you $10-15 every month just for having an account. That's $120-180 per year! The good news is these fees are often waivable if you meet certain requirements like:

Maintaining a minimum balance (often $500-1,500)

Setting up direct deposit

Being under 25 (student accounts rock!)

Having multiple accounts with the same bank

ATM Fees: The $3 That Adds Up Fast

Using an out-of-network ATM can cost you $2-5 per transaction – and that's just YOUR bank's fee. The ATM owner might charge another $2-3. Use the wrong ATM twice a week and you're spending $200+ per year just to access your own money.

Money Tip: Look for banks with large ATM networks or ones that reimburse ATM fees. Many online banks will refund all ATM fees, which is honestly amazing. Some traditional banks have rewards programs that waive ATM fees.

Overdraft Fees: The $35 Mistake

This is the big one that catches young people. Spend more than you have in your account, and many banks will "helpfully" approve and cover the transaction – then charge you $35 for the favor. Buy a $4 coffee with $2 in your account? That coffee just cost you $39.

The sneaky part is that banks often process larger transactions first, which can trigger multiple overdraft fees in one day. Imagine having $100 in your account and making these purchases: $3 coffee, $8 lunch, $95 textbook. If they process the $95 first, then both smaller purchases overdraft – that's $70 in fees on top of your $106 in purchases.

The explanation above should clarify overdraft fees, but following guidance from the CFPB, many banks have recently eliminated or significantly reduced overdraft fees, which historically could be as high as $35.

Interest Rates: Making Your Money Work (A Little)

Let's be honest – you're not going to get rich off savings account interest right now. But understanding how it works sets you up for bigger financial wins later.

APY: The Number That Actually Matters

APY stands for Annual Percentage Yield, and it's the real rate of return you'll earn. Don't get confused by "interest rate" versus APY – always look at the APY because it includes compounding.

At any given time, you will find that high-yield savings accounts from online banks offer significantly higher APY—often many times higher— than the accounts at traditional brick-and-mortar banks.

Financial Reality: Even a high-yield savings account paying 4% APY will only earn you $40 per year on $1,000. That's not life-changing money, but it's better than earning $1 per year at a traditional bank.

Compound Interest: Your Future Best Friend

Here's the cool part about interest – you earn money on your money, then you earn money on that money too. It's like a snowball effect, but with cash.

Let's say you save $50 per month in an account earning 4% APY:

After 1 year: $610 (you saved $600, earned $10)

After 5 years: $3,306 (you saved $3,000, earned $306)

After 10 years: $7,347 (you saved $6,000, earned $1,347)

The longer you leave it alone, the more powerful it becomes. Compound interest is often called the "eighth wonder of the world" because of its ability to generate exponential growth over time, especially when applied to investments. Albert Einstein is famously quoted as saying, "He who understands it, earns it. He who doesn't, pays it," highlighting both its potential for wealth accumulation and the consequences of ignoring it.

Banking Features: The Stuff That Actually Matters Daily

Mobile Apps: Your Bank in Your Pocket

Your bank's app is probably going to be how you interact with your money 90% of the time. Look for apps that let you:

Check balances and transaction history

Deposit checks by taking photos

Transfer money between accounts

Pay bills

Find ATMs

Set up account alerts

Money Tip: *Download a few banking apps and play around with the demos before choosing. If the app is confusing or slow, imagine dealing with that frustration every day.*

ATM Networks: Access Without Fees

Some banks have thousands of ATMs, others have dozens. Check out:

How many ATMs are near your home, school, and work

Whether they're part of networks like Allpoint or MoneyPass

If the bank reimburses out-of-network ATM fees

Customer Service: When Things Go Wrong

You will eventually need to call your bank. Maybe there's a weird charge, maybe you lost your debit card, maybe you need to dispute a transaction. Look for:

24/7 phone support

Live chat options

Good reviews for actually helping customers

Local branches if you prefer face-to-face help

Online vs Traditional Banking

Online Banking: The Digital Revolution

Online banks are like the Netflix of banking – they cut out the expensive overhead and pass the savings on to you. Here's what makes them awesome:

Higher Interest Rates

Without paying for fancy buildings and tons of employees, online banks can offer savings rates that are often 10-100 times higher than traditional banks. We're talking 4-5% APY versus 0.01% APY.

Lower (or No) Fees

Many online banks have:

No monthly maintenance fees

No minimum balance requirements

ATM fee reimbursements

Free overdraft protection options

24/7 Access

Everything happens through your phone or computer, which means you can bank at 2 AM in your pajamas. Mobile check deposits, instant transfers, bill pay – it's all there whenever you need it.

Money Tip: Online banks are perfect for savings accounts because you're not accessing that money daily anyway. The higher interest rates can really add up over time.

Traditional Banking: The Old School Advantage

Brick-and-mortar banks aren't dead yet, and here's why some people still love them:

Face-to-Face Service

Sometimes you need to talk to a human being who can actually help solve complex problems. Traditional banks offer:

In-person account opening (helpful if you're under 18)

Notary services

Cashier's checks and money orders

Complex problem resolution

Large ATM Networks

Big banks like Chase, Bank of America, and Wells Fargo have ATMs everywhere. If you travel a lot or live in a small town, this convenience factor is huge.

Full-Service Banking

Traditional banks can handle everything from basic checking to mortgages to business accounts. As your financial life gets more complex, having everything in one place can be convenient.

Local Community Connection

Credit unions and community banks often offer:

Lower loan rates

More flexible lending criteria

Community involvement

Personalized service

The Hybrid Approach: Best of Both Worlds

Here's a strategy that many financially savvy people use: keep your checking account at a traditional bank for convenience, but put your savings at an online bank for better rates.

For example:

Local checking account: Easy ATM access, direct deposit, bill pay

Online savings account: High interest rates, automatic transfers from checking

This way, you get the convenience of local banking for daily transactions and the higher returns of online banking for your savings goals.

Money Tip: Many online banks partner with ATM networks, so you might have more fee-free ATM access than you think. Check their ATM locator before assuming you'll be stuck with fees.

Security: Keeping Your Money Safe

Whether you choose online or traditional banking, security should be a top priority:

FDIC Insurance

This is non-negotiable. Make sure any bank you choose is FDIC insured, which means the government backs your deposits up to $250,000. If the bank fails, you get your money back.

Encryption and Security Features

Look for:

Two-factor authentication

Account alerts for transactions

The ability to instantly freeze your debit card

Fraud monitoring and protection

Financial Reality: Online banks are generally just as secure as traditional banks – sometimes more so because they invest heavily in cybersecurity. The bigger risk is usually your own behavior (using weak passwords, banking on public WiFi, etc.).

Banking Services That Make Life Easier

Debit Cards: Your Gateway to Spending

Your debit card is probably going to be your most-used financial tool, so let's make sure you understand how to use it wisely.

PIN vs Signature Transactions

When you use your debit card, you usually have two options:

PIN (debit): You enter your PIN, money comes directly from checking

Signature (credit): You sign or hit "credit," but money still comes from checking

The difference matters because:

PIN transactions usually process faster

Signature transactions might have better fraud protection

Some merchants prefer one over the other

Fees might be different (though most banks don't charge extra anymore)

Daily Spending Limits

Most debit cards have daily limits like:

$500-1,500 for purchases

$300-800 for ATM withdrawals

These limits protect you from fraud, but they can be inconvenient if you need to make a large purchase. You can usually call your bank to temporarily increase limits.

Money Tip: If you're planning a big purchase or traveling, call your bank ahead of time. Nothing's worse than having your card declined when you're trying to buy textbooks or pay for gas in another state.

Overdraft Protection Options

You typically have three choices:

No protection: Card gets declined if you don't have enough money

Link to savings: Money automatically transfers from savings to cover purchases

Overdraft coverage: Bank covers the transaction and charges you a fee

Option 1 might seem embarrassing, but it's often the cheapest. Option 2 is good if you keep money in savings. Option 3 is expensive and should be avoided.

Mobile Banking: Your Financial Command Center

Banking apps have gotten incredibly powerful. Here's what you should be using:

Mobile Check Deposits

Take a photo of the front and back of a check, and it deposits into your account. Most banks make funds available the next business day, though they might hold large checks longer.

Money Tip: Endorse checks with "For Mobile Deposit Only" and your signature to prevent fraud if someone finds the check later.

Bill Pay and Transfers

Set up payees once, then pay bills with a few taps. You can:

Pay one-time bills

Set up recurring payments

Schedule future payments

Transfer money between your accounts instantly

Account Alerts

Set up notifications for:

Low balances (so you don't overdraft)

Large transactions (fraud protection)

Direct deposits (know when you get paid)

Bill due dates (avoid late fees)

Financial Reality: Mobile banking is incredibly convenient, but always use secure WiFi or cellular data. Public WiFi at coffee shops is not the place to check your bank balance.

Automatic Transfers: Set It and Forget It

Automation is your secret weapon for building good financial habits without thinking about it.

Savings Automation

Set up automatic transfers from checking to savings:

Right after payday (so you save before you spend)

Small amounts weekly ($25/week = $1,300/year)

Round-up programs that save your spare change

Direct Deposit

Get your paycheck deposited automatically. Many banks offer perks like:

Waived monthly fees

Early access to funds (sometimes 1-2 days early)

Automatic splitting between checking and savings

Automatic Bill Pay

Set up recurring bills like:

Phone and utilities

Streaming services

Insurance payments

Minimum credit card payments (if you have cards)

Money Tip: Start small with automation. Maybe save $25 per week automatically, then increase it as you get comfortable with your cash flow.

Building Banking Relationships That Actually Help You

Customer Service: Getting the Help You Need

Your bank should feel like a partner, not an adversary. Here's how to build a relationship that works:

Questions to Ask When Opening Accounts

Don't just sign papers – ask:

"What fees might I encounter and how can I avoid them?"

"What's the best way to contact customer service?"

"Are there student discounts or special programs for my age?"

"How can I increase my ATM access without fees?"

"What happens if I need to dispute a transaction?"

Problem Resolution

When issues come up (and they will), approach them strategically:

Start with the mobile app or website chat

Call customer service during business hours when possible

Be polite but persistent

Ask to speak to a supervisor if needed

Document everything (dates, names, reference numbers)

Money Tip: If you're a good customer (no overdrafts, regular deposits, multiple accounts), banks will often waive fees or provide better service. Don't be afraid to mention your customer history when asking for help.

Financial Education: Learning While You Bank

Many banks offer resources that can help you level up your financial game:

Free Workshops and Webinars

Topics might include:

Budgeting basics

Credit building

Home buying preparation

Investment fundamentals

Online Resources

Bank websites often have:

Financial calculators

Educational articles

Budgeting tools

Goal-setting features

Financial Counseling

Some banks and credit unions offer free one-on-one financial counseling to help with:

Debt management

Savings strategies

Credit improvement

Financial goal planning

Product Evolution: Growing With Your Bank

Your banking needs will change as your life evolves. Here's how that typically looks:

High School/First Job

Basic checking and savings

Debit card

Mobile banking

Small emergency fund

College Years

Student checking accounts

Higher savings goals

Maybe a first credit card

Student loan management

First Real Job

Higher balance accounts

Investment account options

Better credit products

Insurance products

> ***Money Tip:*** *Stick with banks that can grow with you, but don't be afraid to switch if you find better deals elsewhere. Your bank should earn your loyalty, not expect it.*

Finally, your banking history matters more than you might think:

banks can track everything and how you spend your money is a testament of how you are as a person and as a potential borrower. They track how long you've been a customer, overdraft frequency, average account balance, types of expenses, and whether you've maintained your account responsibly over time. This history can influence whether you get approved for loans, qualify for fee waivers, or receive better interest rates down the line. Building a solid relationship with your bank now—even if you're only depositing a part-time paycheck—can create opportunities later when you're applying for a car loan, renting your first apartment, or even starting a business.

So don't treat banking like background noise. Learn the features, understand the fine print, and use the tools available to you. Banks can feel daunting at first, but they are an excellent mechanism to grow your wealth.

Chapter 4: Building Credit History

You're 18, just graduated high school, and suddenly everyone's talking about "building credit." Your parents mention it. Your older cousin warns you about it. That financial aid counselor at college orientation definitely said something about it. But honestly? You have no clue what any of it means, and you're kind of afraid to ask because it sounds super complicated and very adult-y.

Here's the truth: **credit is basically your financial reputation**, and just like your social media presence, it follows you everywhere. The difference? Your credit score can determine whether you get that apartment you want, the car loan you need, or even some jobs you're applying for. Yeah, it's that important.

But don't panic! Building good credit isn't some mysterious adult skill that requires a business degree. It's actually pretty straightforward once you understand the basics, and the sooner you start, the better off you'll be. Think of this chapter as your crash course in becoming credit-smart without the stress.

Understanding Credit Scores

Let's start with the basics: **what exactly is a credit score?** Think of it as your financial GPA – a three-digit number that tells lenders how reliable you are with borrowed money. Just like your GPA reflects your academic performance, your credit score reflects your history of paying back what you owe.

The Credit Score Breakdown

The most common credit score is called a **FICO score**, and it ranges from 300 to 850. Here's how the ranges break down:

300-579: Poor (Ouch – this makes borrowing really expensive)

580-669: Fair (Not great, but you're getting somewhere)

670-739: Good (Nice! Most lenders will work with you)

740-850: Excellent (You're basically a financial rockstar)

Financial Reality: Most people don't start with perfect credit – that's totally normal! When you're just starting out, you literally have no credit history, which means you have no score at all. It's like being a transfer student with no GPA yet.

What Actually Affects Your Credit Score

Your credit score isn't some random number that changes based on the weather. It's calculated using five specific factors, and understanding these is like knowing exactly what's going to be on the test:

Payment History (35% of your score)

This is the big one – **do you pay your bills on time?** Even being 30 days late on a payment can ding your score. Think of this as the "reliability" factor. If you borrowed $20 from a friend and took three months to pay them back, would they want to lend to you again? Probably not.

Credit Utilization (30% of your score)

This measures **how much of your available credit you're actually using**. If you have a credit card with a $1,000 limit and you owe $300, your utilization is 30%. Lower is better – ideally under 30%, and even better under 10%.

Money Tip: If your credit limit is $500, try to keep your balance under $150 (that's 30%). If you can keep it under $50, even better!

Length of Credit History (15% of your score)

How long have you had credit accounts? This is why starting early (responsibly!) gives you an advantage. A two-year-old credit card account looks better than a two-month-old one.

Credit Mix (10% of your score)

Do you handle different types of credit responsibly? This includes credit cards, student loans, car loans, etc. Don't stress about this one when you're starting out – it's the least important factor.

New Credit Inquiries (10% of your score)

How often are you applying for new credit? Applying for five credit cards in one month makes you look desperate and risky to lenders.

Getting Your Credit Report

Here's something cool: **you're entitled to a free credit report from each of the three major credit bureaus every year**. The big three are:

Experian
Equifax
TransUnion

Go to **AnnualCreditReport.com** (this is the official government-authorized site) to get your free reports. Pro tip: Don't get all three at once. Space them out every four months so you can monitor your credit throughout the year.

Credit Monitoring Made Easy

You don't have to wait for your annual report to check your credit. There are tons of free tools that let you monitor your score:

Credit Karma (totally free, updates weekly)

Credit Sesame (also free with helpful tips)

Your bank's app (many banks such as Bank of America or Chase now offer free credit score monitoring)

Credit Karma and Credit Sesame use the VantageScore model, which can differ slightly from the FICO score most lenders use.

Money Tip: These free tools are great for monitoring, but the scores might be slightly different from what lenders see. Don't stress about small variations – focus on the overall trends.

First Credit Card Strategies

Okay, so you understand credit scores, but how do you actually start building credit when you have no credit history? It's like that classic job search problem: you need experience to get a job, but you need a job to get experience. Fortunately, there are several ways to break into the credit game.

Secured Credit Cards: Training Wheels for Credit

A **secured credit card** is probably your best first step. Here's how it works: you put down a security deposit (usually $200-$500), and that becomes your credit limit. So if you deposit $300, you get a $300 credit limit.

Why this is genius: You're basically borrowing your own money, so the bank has no risk. But it still reports to credit bureaus like a regular credit card, so you're building real credit history.

Top secured cards for beginners:

Discover it Secured: No annual fee, and they actually give you cash back on purchases

Capital One Platinum Secured: Low deposit options, potential to upgrade to unsecured

Citi Secured Mastercard: Reports to all three credit bureaus

Financial Reality: You'll get your security deposit back when you close the account in good standing or upgrade to an unsecured card. Think of it as a refundable investment in your financial future.

Student Credit Cards: Made for Your Situation

If you're in college, **student credit cards** are designed specifically for people with limited credit history. They typically have:

Lower credit requirements

No annual fees

Educational resources about credit

Sometimes rewards on categories students use (like dining or gas)

Popular student cards:

Discover it Student: Cash back rewards and free credit score monitoring

Capital One Journey Student: Rewards for good grades (seriously!)

Chase Freedom Student: Rotating bonus categories

Money Tip: You'll need to show proof of enrollment and some form of income. That part-time job at the campus bookstore or your summer internship counts!

Becoming an Authorized User

This is like credit training wheels with a safety net. **Ask a parent or family member with good credit to add you as an authorized user** on their credit card account. You get a card with your name on it, but they're ultimately responsible for payments.

The benefits:

You inherit their payment history on that account

It can boost your credit score relatively quickly

You get to practice using credit responsibly

The risks:

If they mess up payments, it hurts your credit too

Some family drama potential if spending gets out of hand

You're not building independent credit management skills

Money Tip: Have an honest conversation about spending limits and expectations before becoming an authorized user. Maybe agree that you'll Venmo them immediately for any purchases you make.

Credit Builder Loans: A Different Approach

Credit builder loans are specifically designed to help people build credit. Here's the unique twist: instead of getting money upfront, you make monthly payments into a savings account, and you get the money at the end.

Companies like **Self** and **Credit Strong** offer these loans. You might pay $25-$150 per month for 12-24 months, and at the end, you get all that money back (minus fees). Meanwhile, your payments are reported to credit bureaus.

Why this works: It shows you can make consistent monthly payments, which is exactly what lenders want to see

Responsible Credit Use

Getting your first credit card is exciting – it feels like free money! But here's where a lot of people (including some adults who should know better) mess up. **Credit isn't free money; it's borrowed money that you have to pay back, usually with interest.**

Payment Timing: The Golden Rule

Here's the most important thing you need to know about credit cards: **pay your full balance every month, on time, every single time.** Not the minimum payment – the full balance.

Why this matters:

You avoid interest charges completely

You build a perfect payment history

You never get trapped in debt

You look like a credit superstar to future lenders

Money Tip: Set up autopay for at least the minimum payment as a safety net, but always aim to pay the full balance. Most credit card apps let you set up autopay in about 30 seconds.

Understanding Interest Rates

If you don't pay your full balance, you'll be charged interest (called APR – Annual Percentage Rate). Credit card interest rates are typically 15-25%, which is pretty high. Here's a reality check:

If you have a $1,000 balance and only pay the minimum each month, it could take you over 4 years to pay it off, and you'd pay hundreds of dollars in interest. That $1,000 shopping spree suddenly costs $1,400+.

Credit Utilization: The 30% Rule

Remember how credit utilization makes up 30% of your credit score? **Keep your credit card balances under 30% of your credit limit, and ideally under 10%.**

Let's say you have a $1,000 credit limit:

Good: Using $300 or less (30% utilization)
Better: Using $100 or less (10% utilization)
Avoid: Using $800+ (80% utilization – this hurts your score)

Money Tip: You can actually pay down your balance before your statement closes to keep utilization low. If you spent $400 but pay $300 before the statement date, only $100 gets reported to credit bureaus.

The Multiple Cards Strategy (Advanced Move)

Once you have some credit history, having multiple cards can actually help your utilization ratio. If you have two cards with $1,000 limits each, you have $2,000 total available credit. Spending $300 across both cards is only 15% utilization instead of 30%.

Financial Reality: Only do this if you're already managing one card perfectly. More cards mean more opportunities to mess up if you're not disciplined.

Credit Monitoring: Stay on Top of Your Game

Check your credit card statements every month. I know, I know – it sounds boring. But this is how you catch fraud early and make sure everything looks right.

What to look for:

Charges you don't recognize

Incorrect amounts

Payments not showing up

Changes to your credit limit or interest rate

Most credit card apps send you notifications for every transaction, which makes monitoring way easier. Turn on those notifications!

Dispute Process

If you find an error or fraudulent charge, **dispute it immediately**. Most credit card companies have zero fraud liability, meaning you won't be responsible for fraudulent charges if you report them quickly.

Money Tip: Take a screenshot or save documentation of any disputes. Most can be handled through your credit card app or website.

Building Credit Mix Over Time

As you get older and your financial life gets more complex, you'll naturally develop a **credit mix** – different types of credit accounts. This might include:

Credit cards (what you're starting with)

Student loans (if you go to college)

Auto loans (when you buy a car)

Mortgage (when you buy a house someday)

Don't rush to get different types of credit just for the sake of it. Let your credit mix develop naturally as your life requires different types of financing.

Credit Mistakes to Avoid

Let's talk about the credit mistakes that can haunt you for years. The good news? Now that you know about them, you can avoid them completely.

Late Payments: The Credit Score Killer

A payment that's 30+ days late gets reported to credit bureaus and can drop your credit score by 60-100 points. Yeah, it's that serious.

How to avoid this:

Set up autopay for at least the minimum payment

Use calendar reminders on your phone

Check your due dates regularly (they can change)

Pay a few days early to account for processing time

Payment Timing Confusion

Here's something that trips up a lot of people: **your payment due date and your statement closing date are different.**

Statement closing date: When your monthly statement is generated

Payment due date: When your payment is due (usually 21-25 days after statement closes)

You want to pay your full balance by the due date to avoid interest and late fees.

Maxing Out Cards: The Utilization Trap

Using all or most of your available credit hurts your credit score, even if you pay it off every month. High utilization makes you look risky to lenders.

Instead of maxing out credit cards:

Build an emergency fund for unexpected expenses

Request a credit limit increase if you need more spending power

Consider a second card if you're managing your first one perfectly

Financial Reality: If you're consistently maxing out your credit cards, you're probably spending more than you can afford. This is a sign to revisit your budget and spending habits.

Closing Old Cards: The History Mistake

Don't close your oldest credit cards, especially if they don't have annual fees. Here's why:

Credit history length: Older accounts help your credit score

Available credit: Closing cards reduces your total credit limit, which can increase your utilization ratio

Credit mix: Fewer accounts can hurt your credit mix

What to do with old cards:

Keep them open but use them occasionally (maybe once every few months)

Pay them off immediately

Store them somewhere safe so you're not tempted to overspend

Money Tip: If an old card has a high annual fee and you're not using the benefits, then it might make sense to close it. But if it's free, keep it open.

Too Many Applications: The Inquiry Problem

Every time you apply for credit, the lender does a **hard inquiry** on your credit report. Too many hard inquiries in a short time period can hurt your credit score and make you look desperate to lenders.

Smart application strategy:

Space out credit applications by at least 6 months

Only apply for credit you actually need

Do your research first so you're likely to get approved

Avoid store credit cards unless the benefits are really worth it

Financial Reality: One or two hard inquiries won't significantly hurt your score, but five applications in two months definitely will.

The Store Credit Card Trap

"Save 20% today if you open our store credit card!" Sounds tempting, right? But store credit cards often have:

Very high interest rates (25%+ is common)

Low credit limits

Limited usefulness (only at that store)

Aggressive marketing for more spending

Money Tip: If you're going to make a large purchase anyway and you'll pay it off immediately, a store card discount might be worth it. But don't open store cards just for small savings.

Money Moves: Your Credit Building Action Plan

Alright, let's turn all this knowledge into action. Here's your step-by-step plan for building awesome credit:

Week 1: Assessment and Setup

Check if you have any credit history by signing up for Credit Karma or your bank's credit monitoring

If you have no credit history, research secured credit cards or talk to your parents about becoming an authorized user

If you already have some credit, review your current accounts and payment history

Week 2: Get Your First Credit Account

Apply for your first credit card (secured card, student card, or become an authorized user)

Set up autopay for at least the minimum payment as soon as you get the card

Download your credit card's mobile app and turn on transaction notifications

Month 1: Establish Good Habits

Make small purchases you would make anyway (gas, groceries, subscription services)

Pay off the full balance before the due date

Check your statement when it comes in to make sure everything looks right

Months 2-6: Build Consistency

10. **Continue making on-time payments** for your full balance every month

11. **Keep your utilization under 30%** (ideally under 10%)

12. **Monitor your credit score** monthly to see your progress

Month 6+: Level Up

13. **Consider requesting a credit limit increase** if you've been responsible

14. **If you have a secured card,** ask about upgrading to an unsecured card. This upgrade can boost your credit score, improve your credit mix, and get your security deposit refunded. It's one of the first signs that lenders trust you more—and that's a great milestone to hit.

Remember: credit is a long game. It's not about trying to "hack" the system or rush to an 800 score overnight. It's about building consistent, smart habits that prove you're financially responsible. Pay on time, don't overextend yourself, and check in on your progress.

Credit can open major doors—apartments, cars, even job offers. And the earlier you start building it wisely, the more freedom and opportunity you'll have down the road.

Chapter 5: Saving and Investment Basics

You just got your first "real" paycheck from your part-time job, and after doing a little happy dance, you're wondering what to do with this newfound wealth. Your friends are posting about their latest shopping hauls, there's a concert you're dying to attend, and don't even get me started on that gaming setup you've been eyeing. But somewhere in the back of your mind, you're hearing your parents' voices talking about "saving for the future" and "being responsible with money."

Here's the thing – they're not wrong, but they're also not explaining it in a way that makes sense for your life right now. Let's talk about saving and investing like the financial game-changers they actually are, not like some boring adult lecture you're trying to avoid.

Emergency Fund Building

Why You Need an Emergency Fund (Yes, Even as a Teen)

Let's start with a reality check: emergencies don't care about your age, your bank balance, or whether you're "just a teenager." I learned this the hard way when my car decided to break down the week before my SATs. Suddenly, I needed $800 for repairs, and guess what? My $47 checking account balance wasn't going to cut it.

An **emergency fund** is basically your financial superhero cape – it's there to save the day when life throws you a curveball. And trust me, life LOVES throwing curveballs.

> **Money Tip:** *Think of your emergency fund as buying yourself peace of mind. It's the difference between a stressful situation and a manageable inconvenience.*

What Actually Counts as an Emergency?

Before we dive into building this fund, let's get clear on what actually qualifies as an emergency. Spoiler alert: wanting the latest iPhone doesn't make the cut.

Real emergencies include:

Job loss (yes, even losing your part-time job counts)

Medical bills not covered by insurance

Car repairs that you need to get to work or school

Unexpected family situations that require financial help

Essential item replacements (like your laptop dying during finals week)

Financial Reality: That concert ticket you forgot to buy until the last minute? Not an emergency. Your laptop crashing the night before a major project is due? Definitely an emergency.

How Much Should You Save?

The traditional advice is to save 3-6 months of expenses, but let's be realistic about where you are in life. If you're living at home and your biggest monthly expense is your Spotify subscription, you don't need thousands of dollars sitting around.

Here's a more realistic approach:

Starting Out (Ages 13-17, Living at Home)
Target: $500-$1,000

This covers:

Car repairs or maintenance

Replacing essential items (phone, laptop)

Helping with unexpected family expenses

Small medical copays or prescriptions

Young Adults (Ages 18-25, More Independent)
Target: $1,000-$3,000 initially, building toward 3-6 months of expenses

This covers:

Rent for a month or two

Larger car repairs

Medical emergencies

Job loss buffer while you find new work

Where to Keep Your Emergency Fund

Your emergency fund needs to be easily accessible but not so accessible that you're tempted to spend it on non-emergencies. Here are your best options:

High-Yield Online Savings Accounts

These are your best friend for emergency funds. They offer:

Higher interest rates than traditional banks (we're talking 4-5% vs. 0.01%)

Easy online access when you need the money

FDIC insurance (your money is protected up to $250,000)

Popular options include:

Marcus by Goldman Sachs

Ally Bank Online Savings

Capital One 360 Performance Savings

Discover Online Savings

Money Market Accounts

These are like savings accounts' slightly more sophisticated cousin:

Usually offer **higher interest rates** than regular savings

May come with **check-writing privileges** for true emergencies

Often require **higher minimum balances**

What NOT to Use

Your checking account (too tempting to spend)

Cash under your mattress (earning zero interest and not FDIC protected)

Investment accounts (values fluctuate, and you might need to sell at a loss)

Automating Your Emergency Fund

The secret to building an emergency fund isn't willpower – it's automation. When you automate your savings, you remove the decision-making (and the temptation to spend) from the equation.

Direct Deposit Split

If your employer offers direct deposit, ask them to split your paycheck:

80-90% goes to your checking account for regular expenses

10-20% goes directly to your emergency fund savings account

Automatic Transfers

Set up automatic transfers from your checking to your emergency fund savings:

Weekly transfers of $10-25 (less noticeable than monthly)

Bi-weekly transfers timed with your paychecks

Monthly transfers of a larger amount if you prefer

Pay Yourself First

This is a game-changing mindset shift. Instead of saving whatever's left over (spoiler: there's usually nothing left), you save first and spend what remains.

> *Money Tip: Start small with automation. Even $5 per week adds up to $260 per year, and you probably won't even notice it missing from your checking account.*

Short-term Savings Goals

Making Saving Actually Exciting

Let's be honest – saving money for some vague "future emergency" isn't exactly thrilling. But saving for that spring break trip with your friends? That car you've been dreaming about? Your first apartment? Now we're talking.

Short-term savings goals are your financial motivation fuel. They give you something concrete to work toward and help you build the saving habit without feeling like you're depriving yourself forever.

Setting Goals That Actually Work

The difference between wishful thinking and actual goal achievement comes down to how you set up your goals. Here's the formula that actually works:

The SMART Goals Framework

Specific: "I want to buy a car" vs. "I want to save $8,000 for a 2019 Honda Civic"

Measurable: You can track your progress with actual numbers

Achievable: Realistic based on your income and timeline

Relevant: Something you actually want, not what others think you should want

Time-bound: Has a specific deadline

Example Goal Breakdown

Goal: Save $2,000 for a spring break trip to Florida

Timeline: 8 months

Monthly savings needed: $250

Weekly savings needed: $62.50

If you work 15 hours/week at $12/hour: You need to save about 35% of your income

Financial Reality: If that breakdown feels impossible, adjust either the goal amount, the timeline, or look for ways to increase your income. There's no shame in being realistic.

Common Short-term Savings Goals

Car Purchase ($3,000-$15,000)

    Used car: $3,000-$8,000

    Newer used car: $8,000-$15,000

    Timeline: 1-3 years depending on your income

College Expenses ($500-$5,000 per year)

    Textbooks and supplies: $500-$1,200 per year

    Room and board supplements: $2,000-$5,000

    Study abroad programs: $3,000-$10,000

First Apartment ($2,000-$5,000)

    Security deposit: Usually 1-2 months' rent

    First month's rent: $500-$2,000 depending on location

    Basic furniture and supplies: $1,000-$3,000

Travel and Experiences ($500-$3,000)

    Weekend trips: $200-$500

    Spring break: $800-$2,500

    Concert/festival tickets: $100-$500

Best Savings Vehicles for Short-term Goals

High-Yield Savings Accounts

    Perfect for goals 6 months to 2 years away:

    Liquidity: Access your money anytime

    Safety: FDIC insured

Growth: 4-5% annual interest

Certificates of Deposit (CDs)

Great for goals with fixed timelines:

Higher rates: Often 0.5-1% higher than savings accounts

Fixed terms: 6 months to 5 years

Penalty for early withdrawal: Makes sure you don't touch the money

Money Tip: Only use CDs if you're 100% sure you won't need the money before the term ends. The penalties can eat up your interest gains.

Money Market Accounts

Good middle ground between checking and savings:

Higher interest than regular savings

Limited check writing for when you're ready to make your purchase

Higher minimum balances required

Investment Introduction

Why Investing Isn't Just for Rich Adults

Here's a secret that nobody tells teenagers: the best time to start investing isn't when you're 30 with a "real job" and a mortgage. It's right now, even if you only have $25 to your name.

I know what you're thinking – "I can barely afford gas money, and you want me to invest in the stock market?" But here's the thing: **time is your superpower** when it comes to investing, and you have something that every adult investor wishes they could buy more of – decades ahead of you.

Understanding Risk vs. Return

Let's start with the fundamental rule of investing: **higher risk typically means higher potential return**, but it also means higher potential loss.

Think of it like this:

Keeping cash under your mattress: Zero risk, zero return (actually negative return due to inflation)

High-yield savings account: Very low risk, low return (3-5% annually)

Bonds: Low to moderate risk, moderate return (4-8% annually)

Stock market: Moderate to high risk, higher potential return (historically 10% annually over long periods)

Individual stocks or crypto: High risk, potentially very high returns OR very high losses

Financial Reality: There's no such thing as high returns without risk. Anyone promising you guaranteed high returns is either lying or running a scam.

Assessing Your Risk Tolerance

Your risk tolerance depends on several factors:

Timeline: Money you need in 2 years should be low-risk; money for retirement in 40 years can handle more risk

Financial situation: If losing $500 would be devastating, stick to lower-risk investments

Sleep-at-night factor: If market fluctuations keep you awake, dial back the risk

---

Types of Investments

Stocks

When you buy stock, you're buying a tiny piece of a company. If the company does well, your stock value goes up. If it struggles, your stock value goes down.

Examples:

Apple stock (AAPL)

Microsoft stock (MSFT)

Tesla stock (TSLA)

Pros: Potential for high returns, you own part of companies you believe in

Cons: Can be volatile, individual companies can fail

Bonds

Think of bonds as IOUs. You lend money to a company or government, and they pay you back with interest over time.

Types:

Government bonds: Very safe, lower returns

Corporate bonds: Slightly riskier, higher returns

Municipal bonds: Tax advantages in some cases

Pros: More stable than stocks, regular income payments

Cons: Lower potential returns, inflation risk

Mutual Funds

A mutual fund pools money from many investors to buy a diversified mix of stocks, bonds, or other investments. It's like buying a pre-made smoothie instead of buying all the individual fruits.

Pros: Instant diversification, professional management

Cons: Management fees, less control over specific investments

ETFs (Exchange-Traded Funds)

ETFs are like mutual funds but trade on the stock market like individual stocks. They typically have lower fees than mutual funds.

Popular ETFs:

SPY: Tracks the S&P 500 (500 largest US companies)

VTI: Total US stock market

VXUS: International stocks

Index Funds

These track a specific market index (like the S&P 500) and are designed to match its performance. They're like the "set it and forget it" of investing.

Money Tip: Index funds are often recommended for beginners because they're diversified, low-cost, and don't require you to pick individual stocks.

The Magic of Compound Interest

This is where things get exciting. **Compound interest** is when you earn returns not just on your original investment, but on all the returns you've earned over time. It's like a snowball rolling down a hill, getting bigger and bigger.

Real-World Example

Let's say you invest $1,000 at age 18 and earn an average return of 8% per year:

Age 28: $2,159 (doubled in 10 years)

Age 38: $4,661 (more than quadrupled in 20 years)

Age 48: $10,063 (10x your original investment in 30 years)

Age 58: $21,725 (over 20x in 40 years)

Now let's say your friend waits until age 28 to invest that same $1,000:

Age 58: $10,063

By starting 10 years earlier, you ended up with more than double the money, even though you both invested the exact same amount.

Financial Reality: This is why starting early matters more than starting with a lot of money. Time is your biggest advantage.

A Quick-Look Walk-Through of the Math

Compound growth is just **multiplication on repeat**. The future value (FV) of a single lump-sum grows according to

$$FV = P \times (1 + r)^n$$

Where:

- P = principal (your starting amount)
- r = annual growth rate (as a decimal)
- n = number of compounding periods (years, in this case)

Next is the exact arithmetic behind the story in the chapter.

You start early (age 18, P = $1,000, r = 8%):

1. **After 10 years (age 28)**
   $FV = \$1,000 \times (1 + 0.08)^{10}$
   $= \$1,000 \times 2.159 \approx \textbf{\$2,159}$

2. **After 20 years (age 38)**
   $FV = \$1,000 \times (1 + 0.08)^{20}$
   $= \$1,000 \times 4.661 \approx \textbf{\$4,661}$

3. **After 30 years (age 48) – your friend's return**
   $FV = \$1,000 \times (1 + 0.08)^{30}$
   $= \$1,000 \times 10.063 \approx \textbf{\$10,063}$

4. **After 40 years (age 58)**
   $$FV = \$1{,}000 \times (1 + 0.08)^{40}$$
   $$= \$1{,}000 \times 21.725 \approx \mathbf{\$21{,}725}$$

What just happened?

Each decade, your dollars began earning returns *on top of the returns from all previous decades.* That's why the jump from $10 k to $21 k in the last ten years is larger than the total growth of the first twenty years combined.

Starting just ten years earlier turned the same $1,000 into more than double the ending balance—proof that in personal finance, **time in the market beats timing the market**.

The Rule of 72

Here's a quick way to figure out how long it takes your money to double assuming annual compounding: divide 72 by your *annual return rate*.

8% return: $72 \div 8 = 9$ years to double

10% return: $72 \div 10 = 7.2$ years to double

6% return: $72 \div 6 = 12$ years to double

Why "72" Works—and What's Up with 69 and 70?

Imagine you want a **rule-of-thumb** that tells you, in seconds, how long it takes money to double at any given interest rate. Mathematicians can get the exact answer with logarithms, but that's not exactly bus-ride mental math. So, generations of investors have leaned on a shortcut called the **Rule of 72**:

Where the 72 Comes From

1. **The exact math lands close to 69.**
   If you crunch the numbers precisely, you find that doubling

happens in about **69.3147 percent** divided by the rate. That's because of the natural logarithm of two—no need to memorize it; just know it spits out "roughly 69."

2. **Rounding to 70 is tidier, but 72 is friendlier.**

   o **70** is nice and round, but it divides cleanly only by 2, 5, 7, and 10.

   o **72** divides cleanly by **2, 3, 4, 6, 8, 9, and 12.** Those extra factors make mental division smoother for the interest rates people actually quote: 4%, 6%, 8%, 9%, and so on.

3. **A pinch of practical correction.**
   The "real" doubling time creeps upward if interest is paid more than once a year or if the rate is on the high side. Rounding 69 up to 72 conveniently cancels much of that drift, keeping typical errors within a few months.

Why Do We Sometimes Hear 69 and 70?

- **Rule of 69:**
  Purists like it because it's closest to the true math, especially when interest is **compounded continuously** (a finance-class ideal more than a reality). Great for spreadsheets, clunky for your head.

- **Rule of 70:**
  Economists favor this one for talking about GDP or population growth—a neat "seven-decade" sound bite at 1% growth. It's also slightly more accurate for very low rates (around 2%-5%).

Think of these as three siblings: 69 is the precise scholar, 70 the simple rounder, and 72 the street-smart cousin who's easiest to work with day-to-day.

Take-Away

Use **72** at the coffee shop, **70** if you like round numbers, and **69** when you're fine-tuning in Excel. All three aim to answer the same question: *"Roughly how long until my money doubles?"*—and any one of them gets you close enough to make a smarter decision right now.

Dollar-Cost Averaging

Dollar-cost averaging means investing a fixed amount of money at regular intervals, regardless of market conditions. Instead of trying to time the market (which even professionals struggle with), you invest consistently over time.

How It Works

Let's say you invest $100 every month in an index fund:

Month 1: Stock price is $50, you buy 2 shares

Month 2: Stock price drops to $25, you buy 4 shares

Month 3: Stock price rises to $75, you buy 1.33 shares

Average cost per share: $41.67 instead of $50

By investing consistently, you automatically buy more shares when prices are low and fewer when prices are high.

Money Tip: Dollar-cost averaging removes emotion from investing. You don't have to worry about whether it's a "good time" to invest – you just invest consistently.

Investment Accounts

Where to Actually Put Your Money

Okay, so you're convinced that investing is a good idea, but where do you actually do it? You can't just walk into a store and buy "some stocks, please." You need an investment account, and choosing the right type can save you thousands in taxes over your lifetime.

Taxable Investment Accounts

These are your basic brokerage accounts where you can buy and sell investments. You'll pay taxes on any gains, but you can access your money anytime without penalties.

Best Brokerages for Beginners

- **Fidelity:** No account minimums, excellent research tools, great customer service and app design.
- **Merrill Edge:** No account minimum for their Self-Directed account. Excellent choice if you are a Bank of America customer.
- **Vanguard:** Great for long-term investors focused on index funds
- **Charles Schwab:** Low-cost, strong tools, excellent customer service. They acquired TD Ameritrade.
- **Robinhood:** Easy to use and beginner-focused, but limited account types. Robinhood makes more money the more you trade via Payment-For-Order-Flow, so don't feel the urge to trade just because you get a notification that some security is *hot*.

Whichever platform you choose, the key is to just get started. Open that account, automate your contributions, and let your money grow while you live your life.

Here's the truth: You don't need to be rich to start investing—you need to start investing to eventually become rich (or at least financially free). Saving and investing are two of the most powerful habits you can build. Master them early, and you'll be light-years ahead of most adults.

Chapter 6: Education Financing

You see all your friends posting about their college acceptances, and suddenly it hits you – college costs *how much?* Whether you're a high school junior just starting to think about your future or already knee-deep in college applications, the price tags on higher education can feel absolutely overwhelming. But here's the thing: understanding how education financing works isn't just about surviving college costs – it's about making smart decisions that'll set you up for success without drowning in debt.

Let's break down everything you need to know about paying for your education, from understanding the real costs to making sure you're getting the best bang for your buck. Trust me, a little planning now can save you from major financial stress later.

College Cost Planning

Understanding the Real Price Tag

When colleges throw around numbers like "$50,000 per year," it's easy to panic. But let's break down what you're actually paying for, because understanding these costs helps you make smarter decisions about where and how to spend your education dollars.

Tuition is the big one – this is what you pay for classes, access to professors, and the actual education part. But it's just the beginning. **Room and board** covers your dorm room and meal plan, which can easily add $10,000-15,000 to your annual bill. Then there are **books and supplies** (hello, $300 textbooks that you'll use for one semester), **transportation** costs to get to and from campus, and **personal expenses** like laundry, entertainment, and those late-night pizza runs.

Money Tip: Use college websites' net price calculators to get a realistic estimate of what you'll actually pay after financial aid. The sticker price and your actual cost can be very different!

In-State vs Out-of-State: The Geography Game

Here's where location really matters for your wallet. **Public universities** offer significantly lower tuition rates for in-state students – we're talking potentially $20,000+ difference per year. Why? Your family's tax dollars help fund your state's public universities, so you get the "family discount."

Residency requirements vary by state, but generally, you need to live in a state for at least a year before starting college to qualify for in-state tuition. Some states have reciprocity agreements with neighboring states, offering reduced tuition rates. If you're considering out-of-state schools, make sure the extra cost is worth it for your specific program or career goals.

Financial Reality: That dream school in California might seem worth the extra $25,000 per year, but if you can get a similar education at your state school, you could graduate with $100,000 less debt. That's a house down payment!

Community College: Your Secret Weapon

Let's talk about one of the best-kept secrets in higher education: **community college**. Before you roll your eyes, hear me out. Community colleges offer the same general education requirements as four-year universities at a fraction of the cost – often under $4,000 per year for in-state students.

The **transfer option** is where this gets really smart. You can complete your first two years at community college, then transfer to a four-year university to finish your bachelor's degree. Your diploma will be from the four-year school, but you'll have saved potentially $40,000-60,000 on those first two years.

Community colleges also offer **career programs** and certifications that can lead directly to good-paying jobs. Think nursing, dental hygiene, automotive technology, or computer programming – fields where you can start earning decent money without a four-year degree.

Money Tip: Many community colleges have guaranteed transfer agreements with state universities. You complete specific courses with a certain GPA, and you're automatically accepted as a junior at the four-year school.

Cost Per Credit Hour: Playing the Numbers Game

Understanding **cost per credit hour** helps you make strategic decisions about your course load and graduation timeline. Most colleges charge the same full-time rate whether you take 12 credits or 18 credits per semester. If you can handle the workload, taking extra credits each semester can help you graduate early and save money.

Summer sessions often cost extra, but they can also help you stay on track if you've fallen behind or want to graduate early. **Acceleration options** like AP credits, CLEP exams, or dual enrollment during high school can also reduce your total college costs by letting you skip introductory courses.

Financial Aid Understanding

FAFSA: Your Gateway to Free Money

The **Free Application for Federal Student Aid (FAFSA)** is literally your ticket to free money for college, yet so many students either don't fill it out or mess it up. Let's make sure you're not one of them.

First, it's **completely free** – if a website asks you to pay to fill out the FAFSA, you're on the wrong site. Go to studentaid.gov and nowhere else. You'll need your (and your parents') **tax information** from the previous year, so gather those documents before you start.

Deadline importance cannot be overstated. Federal deadlines are usually in June, but many states and colleges have much earlier deadlines – some as early as February or March. Miss the deadline, miss out on aid. It's that simple.

Here's something many people don't realize: you need to **renew your FAFSA every year**. Your financial situation might change, and aid amounts can vary from year to year. Set a reminder in your phone right now to renew your FAFSA every October.

Money Tip: File your FAFSA as early as possible (it opens October 1st each year). Some aid is distributed on a first-come, first-served basis, so early filers get priority.

Grant Types: The Holy Grail of Financial Aid

Grants are basically free money that you don't have to pay back – which makes them the best type of financial aid. **Pell Grants** are federal need-based grants that can provide up to $7,000+ per year for students from lower-income families. You don't apply separately for Pell Grants; they're automatically considered when you file your FAFSA.

State grants vary widely depending on where you live. Some states offer generous need-based aid, while others focus on merit-based programs. **Institutional grants** come directly from colleges and universities – this is often where applying to schools where your grades and test scores are above average can really pay off.

Need-based aid is determined by your family's financial situation as reported on the FAFSA. Don't assume you won't qualify – middle-class families often receive more aid than they expect, especially at private colleges with large endowments.

Scholarship Search: Beyond the Obvious

Everyone knows about the big, national scholarships, but those are also the most competitive. **Local organizations** – think community foundations, rotary clubs, local businesses – often offer smaller scholarships with much better odds. Your high school counselor probably has a list of these opportunities.

Merit-based scholarships are awarded for academic achievement, special talents, or leadership experience. **Need-based scholarships** consider your financial situation. **Essay competitions** can be time-consuming but are often less competitive than you'd think – many students don't want to write essays, so you're competing against a smaller pool.

Money Tip: Apply for lots of smaller scholarships rather than just focusing on the big ones. Ten $500 scholarships add up to $5,000, and they're often easier to win than one $5,000 scholarship.

Work-Study Programs: Earning While Learning

Federal Work-Study provides part-time jobs for students with financial need, allowing you to earn money to help pay education expenses. These jobs are often on campus and designed to work around your class schedule – think library assistant, dining hall worker, or research assistant.

Campus jobs through work-study programs understand that you're a student first. They typically offer **flexible scheduling** around your classes and exams. Plus, having a job on campus can help you feel more connected to your school community.

The money you earn through work-study doesn't count against you on next year's FAFSA the same way other income does, which is another advantage of these programs.

Student Loan Basics

Federal Loans: Your First Stop

When grants and scholarships don't cover everything (and let's be honest, they usually don't), **federal student loans** should be your next option. They come with better protections and more flexible repayment options than private loans (federal loans account for 92.4% of total loans).

Subsidized federal loans are need-based and don't accrue interest while you're in school at least half-time. **Unsubsidized loans** are available regardless of financial need, but they do accrue interest from the moment they're disbursed. **PLUS loans** are available to parents and graduate students, but they have higher interest rates and fewer protections.

Financial Reality: Federal student loan interest rates are fixed for the life of the loan but are set annually by Congress. For the most current rates, always visit the official Federal Student Aid website at studentaid.gov. Remember, you might be paying this for 10+ years after graduation. Will your career be able to pay this back? In books like *"500 Careers and Salaries"* you can learn more about the expected average salary for the most popular careers.

Private Loans: Proceed with Caution

Private loans from banks, credit unions, or online lenders should be your last resort after you've maxed out federal aid options. They often have **variable interest rates** that can increase over time, and they don't offer the same protections as federal loans.

Most private loans require **good credit** or a **cosigner** (usually a parent or guardian). If your cosigner has financial problems later, it could affect your loan. Some private loans offer cosigner release after you make a certain number of on-time payments, but don't count on it.

Money Tip: If you must take private loans, shop around and compare offers from multiple lenders. Credit unions often offer better rates than big banks.

Understanding Loan Terms

Interest rates determine how much extra you'll pay over the life of your loan. A 1% difference in interest rate can mean thousands of dollars over a 10-year repayment period. **Repayment periods** for federal loans are typically 10 years, but you can extend them to reduce monthly payments (though you'll pay more interest overall).

Grace periods give you time after graduation before you have to start making payments – usually six months for federal loans. **Deferment options** allow you to temporarily stop making payments if you return to school, face economic hardship, or meet other specific criteria.

Borrowing Limits and Responsible Borrowing

Federal loans have **annual limits** (how much you can borrow each year) and **aggregate limits** (total amount you can borrow). For dependent undergraduates, you can borrow $5,500-12,500 per year in federal loans, depending on your year in school.

Responsible borrowing means only taking what you actually need. Just because you're offered $10,000 in loans doesn't mean you have to take it all. Remember, every dollar you borrow will cost you more than a dollar to repay.

Money Tip: Keep a running total of how much you're borrowing each year. Seeing the cumulative amount can help you make better decisions about your spending and borrowing.

Education ROI Analysis

Career Prospects: The Reality Check

Before you commit to a major or a school, do some honest research about **job market prospects** in your field. Use resources like the Bureau of Labor Statistics' Occupational Outlook Handbook to understand salary expectations and growth potential for different careers.

Salary expectations vary dramatically by field. If you're planning to be a social worker (median salary around $61,000), taking on $100,000 in student loans doesn't make financial sense. But if you're going into industrial engineering with a median salary of $101,000 *(Source: Bureau of Labor Statistics)*, you have more room to work with.

Growth potential matters too. Some fields might have lower starting salaries but good advancement opportunities, while others might plateau quickly.

Debt-to-Income Ratio: The Magic Formula

Here's a rule of thumb that can save you from financial disaster: your total student loan debt shouldn't exceed your expected first-year salary after graduation. So if you expect to earn $40,000 per year, don't borrow more than $40,000 total for your entire education.

Your **monthly loan payment** shouldn't exceed 10-15% of your gross monthly income. If you're earning $50,000 per year ($4,167 per month), your student loan payments shouldn't exceed $400-600 per month.

Financial Reality: The average monthly payment on a $30,000 student loan at 5.5% interest over 10 years is about $325. Make sure you can handle that payment on your expected salary.

Alternative Paths: Think Outside the Box

A four-year college degree isn't the only path to a good career. **Trade schools** can prepare you for well-paying jobs in 6 months to 2 years. Electricians, plumbers, and HVAC technicians often earn more than college graduates and have excellent job security.

Professional certifications in fields like IT, digital marketing, or project management can be earned online and cost a fraction of a college degree. **Apprenticeships** combine paid work experience with education, allowing you to earn while you learn.

Online degrees from accredited institutions can significantly reduce costs by eliminating room and board expenses. Just make sure the school is properly accredited and recognized by employers in your field.

Value Assessment: Prestige vs Practicality

The **prestige factor** of attending a famous school can be tempting, but be honest about whether it's worth the extra cost for your specific career goals. If you want to work on Wall Street or become a Supreme Court justice, where you went to school might matter. If you want to be a teacher, nurse, or accountant, it probably doesn't.

Public vs private schools offer different value propositions. Private schools often have smaller class sizes and more resources, but public schools can provide excellent education at a much lower cost. Consider your learning style and career goals when making this decision.

Field-specific considerations matter. Some industries care a lot about where you went to school, while others care more about your skills and experience. Research your intended career path thoroughly before making expensive decisions based on school rankings.

> *Money Tip: Talk to people actually working in your intended field. LinkedIn is great for this – most professionals are happy to answer questions from students about their career paths and what education was most valuable.*

Money Moves

Now that you understand the landscape of education financing, here are some smart moves to make right now:

Start early: Begin researching costs and financial aid options during your sophomore or junior year of high school. The earlier you start, the more options you'll have.

Cast a wide net: Apply to a mix of schools with different price points and aid packages. You can't compare financial aid offers if you don't have multiple offers to compare.

Understand the total cost: Look beyond tuition to understand the full cost of attendance, including living expenses, transportation, and personal costs.

Maximize free money: Apply for every grant and scholarship you're eligible for, no matter how small. Free money is always better than borrowed money.

Borrow federal first: Exhaust federal aid options before considering private loans. Federal loans offer better protections and more flexible repayment options.

Think long-term: Consider your career goals and earning potential when making decisions about how much to borrow and where to attend school.

Your Financial Action Plan

Ready to take control of your education financing? Here's what to do this week:

Create a FAFSA account at studentaid.gov if you haven't already, even if you're not ready to apply yet. Gather the documents you'll need.

Research three schools you're interested in and use their net price calculators to estimate your actual costs after aid.

Make a list of 10 local scholarships you could apply for. Check with your school counselor, local library, and community organizations.

Calculate the debt-to-income ratio for your intended career. Research median starting salaries in your field and determine how much debt you can reasonably handle.

Explore one alternative path to your career goals. Could you start at community college? Are there relevant certifications you could earn? What about trade schools or apprenticeships?

Set up a simple spreadsheet to track college costs, aid offers, and loan amounts as you go through the application process.

Schedule a meeting with your school counselor to discuss your education financing strategy and make sure you're not missing any opportunities.

Remember, paying for education is an investment in your future, but like any investment, you want to make sure you're getting good value for your money. With smart planning and a clear understanding of your options, you can get the education you want without drowning in debt. Your future self will thank you for the time you spend planning now!

Chapter 7: Income Generation and Career Development

You're scrolling through TikTok when you see someone your age showing off their new car, designer clothes, or the apartment they just moved into. Your first thought? "How do they afford all that?" Here's the truth – while some people get financial help from family, many young people today are creating multiple income streams and building careers earlier than ever before. The best part? You can totally do this too, and you don't need to wait until you're "older" to start building real wealth.

Let's talk about turning your time, skills, and energy into actual money – and not just surviving paycheck to paycheck, but thriving and building toward the future you want.

Part-time Job Strategies

Finding Your First Real Job

Getting your first "real" job (you know, the kind with a W-2 form and everything) can feel intimidating, but it's honestly one of the best financial moves you can make. Not just for the money – though that's obviously important – but for all the skills and experience you'll gain that'll pay off for years to come.

The Job Landscape for Young People

Let's break down the most common job types and what they can offer you:

Retail Jobs are everywhere and usually hiring. Yes, dealing with customers can be challenging (and sometimes downright wild), but you'll learn customer service skills that are valuable in literally every career. Plus, many retail jobs offer employee discounts, flexible scheduling, and opportunities to move up to supervisor or management roles pretty quickly.

Food Service might seem basic, but the skills you learn are incredible. You'll master multitasking, working under pressure, teamwork, and handling money. Restaurant jobs often come with tips (hello, cash in your pocket every shift!), and the experience teaches you work ethic that employers in other industries really respect.

Tutoring is perfect if you're good at any subject – and I mean ANY subject. You don't have to be a straight-A student to help someone who's struggling with algebra or needs help writing essays. Tutoring pays well (often \$15-30+ per hour), looks great on college applications, and helps you develop teaching and communication skills.

Campus Jobs (if you're in college) are golden because they understand your schedule and often let you study during downtime. Work-study positions, library jobs, campus tour guide roles, or working in the dining hall can provide steady income without the commute.

Internships might be unpaid or low-paid, but they're investments in your future earning potential. A good internship can lead to job offers, amazing references, and skills that make you way more marketable after graduation.

Building Skills That Actually Matter

Here's something adults don't always tell you: your part-time job is basically a paid training program for life skills. Every shift, you're developing abilities that'll make you more successful and more money throughout your career.

Customer Service Skills teach you how to communicate with all types of people, stay calm under pressure, and solve problems quickly. These skills transfer to literally every job you'll ever have.

Time Management becomes second nature when you're balancing work, school, and having a social life. You'll learn to prioritize, plan ahead, and make the most of your time – skills that'll help you in college and your career.

Communication Skills develop naturally when you're working with teammates, managers, and customers. You'll learn how to ask questions, give updates, handle conflicts, and present yourself professionally.

Responsibility and Reliability might sound boring, but these are the traits that get you promoted, get you better references, and help you stand out from other job candidates later.

Financial Reality: The average part-time job for teens pays between $8-15 per hour, but the real value comes from the experience and skills you gain. Someone who worked part-time through high school and college often earns significantly more in their first post-graduation job than someone with no work experience.

Resume Building That Actually Works

Your part-time job isn't just about the money you earn now – it's about building a resume that opens doors to better opportunities later. Here's how to maximize the resume-building potential of any job:

Document Everything: Keep track of specific accomplishments, not just job duties. Instead of "worked at retail store," write "provided customer service to 50+ customers daily while maintaining 95% customer satisfaction rating" or "trained 3 new employees in POS system and store procedures."

Ask for Increasing Responsibility: Once you've mastered your basic job duties, ask your manager if you can take on additional responsibilities. Maybe you can help with inventory, train new employees, handle social media, or assist with scheduling. These extra duties become great resume bullets.

Build References: Your managers and coworkers can become valuable references for future jobs, college applications, or scholarship applications. Be professional, reliable, and helpful, and don't be afraid to ask for LinkedIn recommendations or reference letters when you leave.

Connect Jobs to Career Goals: Even if your part-time job seems unrelated to your future career, you can usually find connections. Retail teaches sales skills, food service teaches operations management, tutoring shows leadership abilities – frame your experience in ways that support your long-term goals.

Managing Your Income Like a Pro

Getting that first paycheck is exciting, but managing your income properly from day one sets you up for financial success throughout your life.

Understanding Taxes: Your paycheck is going to be smaller than your hourly wage times hours worked, and that's because of taxes. Federal income tax, state income tax (in most states), Social Security, and Medicare taxes all come out of your paycheck. This isn't the government stealing from you – it's how we fund public services, and you'll get some of it back when you file your tax return.

Work-Study Balance: It's tempting to work as many hours as possible when you first start earning money, but don't let work hurt your grades or your health. Most financial experts recommend high school students work no more than 15-20 hours per week during the school year, and college students should generally cap it at 20-25 hours.

Career Planning: Use your part-time job as a way to explore career interests. Love the fast-paced environment of a restaurant? Maybe you're interested in hospitality management. Enjoy helping customers solve problems in retail? Consider sales or customer success roles. Hate your job? That's valuable information too – now you know what you DON'T want to do long-term.

Side Hustle Development

Welcome to the Gig Economy

If traditional part-time jobs don't fit your schedule or personality, welcome to the gig economy – where you can literally make money from your phone, set your own hours, and potentially earn more than traditional jobs. The key word here is "potentially" – side hustles can be amazing, but they require more self-discipline and business thinking than regular jobs.

Financial Reality: Side hustles can be incredibly lucrative, but income is usually inconsistent, you'll pay more in taxes (since you're essentially self-employed), and you won't get benefits like health insurance or paid time off. They're best when combined with other income sources or when you're building toward something bigger.

Gig Economy Opportunities

Rideshare and Delivery: If you're 18+ with a car, apps like Uber, Lyft, DoorDash, and Uber Eats can provide flexible income. You can literally work whenever you want, and in busy areas, you can make $15-25+ per hour. Just remember to factor in gas, car maintenance, and taxes when calculating your real earnings.

Task-Based Work: TaskRabbit, Handy, and similar apps let you get paid for skills like furniture assembly, moving help, handyman work, or cleaning. If you're good with your hands or don't mind physical work, these can pay really well – often $20-40+ per hour.

Freelance Services: Fiverr, Upwork, and similar platforms let you sell basically any skill. Good at writing? Sell blog posts or social media content. Know Photoshop? Offer graphic design services. Speak multiple languages? Offer translation services. The key is starting with competitive prices to build reviews, then raising your rates as you gain experience.

Online Opportunities That Actually Work

Content Creation: YouTube, TikTok, Instagram, and other platforms can generate income through ad revenue, sponsorships, and affiliate marketing. But here's the real talk – building a following takes time, and most content creators don't make significant money for months or years. Treat this as a long-term investment, not a quick money grab.

Social Media Management: Many small businesses need help with their social media but can't afford big marketing agencies. If you understand Instagram, TikTok, Facebook, and other platforms, you can offer to manage accounts for local businesses. Start by offering services to family friends or local businesses you frequent.

Virtual Assistant Work: Busy entrepreneurs and small business owners need help with email management, appointment scheduling, data entry, and other administrative tasks. Websites like Belay, Time Etc, and Fancy Hands hire virtual assistants, often with flexible schedules perfect for students.

> *Money Tip: When starting any online side hustle, create a separate email address and keep detailed records of all income and expenses. You'll need this information for taxes, and it helps you track which activities are actually profitable.*

Local Service Opportunities

Sometimes the best opportunities are right in your neighborhood. Local services often pay well, build great relationships, and can grow into significant businesses.

Pet Services: Dog walking, pet sitting, and pet grooming are in huge demand. Apps like Rover and Wag make it easy to connect with pet owners, but you can also build a client base through word-of-mouth in your neighborhood. Pet sitting can pay $25-75+ per day, and regular dog walking clients provide steady weekly income.

Tutoring and Teaching: You don't need to be a genius to tutor – you just need to be better at a subject than the person you're helping. Elementary and middle school students often need help with basic math, reading, or writing. High school students might need help with specific subjects you excel in. Music lessons, art instruction, or teaching skills like coding can also be lucrative.

Home and Yard Services: Lawn mowing, snow shoveling, house cleaning, organizing, and basic handyman work are always in demand. These services often pay $15-30+ per hour, and satisfied customers become regular clients who provide steady income.

Creative Ventures

If you have creative skills, there are more opportunities than ever to monetize your talents.

Art and Design: Sell original artwork on Etsy, create custom designs for t-shirts through Printful or Teespring, offer logo design services, or sell digital art and designs. Social media makes it easier than ever to showcase your work and find customers.

Music and Performance: Offer music lessons, perform at local events, create custom songs for special occasions, or sell your music on platforms like Spotify and Apple Music. You can also make money through live streaming performances on platforms like Twitch or YouTube.

Photography: Event photography, portrait sessions, product photography for small businesses, or stock photography can all generate income. Start by offering discounted services to build a portfolio, then raise your rates as your skills and reputation grow.

Crafts and Handmade Items: If you enjoy making things, platforms like Etsy, Facebook Marketplace, and local craft fairs provide opportunities to sell handmade items. Jewelry, clothing, home decor, and personalized gifts are popular categories.

Career Investment

Thinking Beyond Your Next Paycheck

Here's where we separate people who just work jobs from people who build careers. Career investment means spending time, energy, and sometimes money now to increase your earning potential later. It's like compound interest, but for your professional life – small investments now can lead to dramatically higher income over time.

Financial Reality: The average college graduate earns about $78,000 per year, while the average high school graduate earns about $45,000. But here's what's even more interesting – college graduates with internship experience, relevant skills, and professional networks often start at $60,000-90,000+, while those without these advantages might start closer to $40,000-50,000.

Skill Development That Pays Off

The job market changes fast, but certain skills remain valuable across industries and economic conditions. Investing in these skills now can significantly boost your earning potential.

High-Value Skills for Young People

Digital Marketing: Understanding social media marketing, email marketing, search engine optimization (SEO), and online advertising is valuable in almost every industry. Free resources like Google's Digital Marketing courses, HubSpot Academy, and YouTube tutorials can teach you these skills.

Data Analysis: Basic skills in Excel, Google Sheets, and data visualization are in demand across industries. More advanced skills in SQL, Python, or Tableau can command premium salaries. Many of these skills can be learned through free online courses.

Communication and Writing: Strong written and verbal communication skills never go out of style. Practice through blogging, creating content, giving presentations, or joining organizations like Toastmasters.

Project Management: Learning to organize tasks, manage timelines, and coordinate with team members is valuable in any career. You can get certified in project management methodologies and use free tools like Trello or Asana to practice.

Money Tip: Focus on skills that combine technology with human elements. While AI and automation are changing the job market, skills that require creativity, emotional intelligence, and complex problem-solving remain in high demand.

Learning Resources That Don't Break the Bank

Free Online Courses: Coursera, edX, Khan Academy, and YouTube offer thousands of free courses on everything from coding to business skills. While certificates might cost money, you can often audit courses for free and gain the knowledge.

Library Resources: Your local library likely offers free access to online learning platforms like LinkedIn Learning, Lynda.com, or Skillshare. Many libraries also host workshops and career development events.

Professional Certifications: Industry certifications in areas like digital marketing (Google Ads, Facebook Blueprint), project management (PMP, Scrum), or technology (Microsoft Office, Adobe Creative Suite) can significantly boost your resume and earning potential.

Networking Without Being Weird About It

Networking sounds intimidating and maybe a little fake, but it's really just about building genuine relationships with people in fields you're interested in. Most successful people are happy to help young people who are genuinely interested in learning and growing.

Building Your Professional Network

LinkedIn Strategy: Create a professional LinkedIn profile with a good photo, clear headline, and summary of your goals and interests. Connect with classmates, coworkers, family friends, and professionals you meet. Share interesting articles and comment thoughtfully on others' posts.

Professional Organizations: Many industries have professional organizations with student memberships at discounted rates. These organizations often host networking events, offer mentorship programs, and provide job boards exclusive to members.

Career Fairs and Industry Events: Attend career fairs at your school and local industry events. Come prepared with questions about the industry, not just requests for jobs. People remember students who show genuine interest in learning about their field.

Informational Interviews: Reach out to professionals in fields you're interested in and ask for 15-20 minutes of their time to learn about their career path. Most people are flattered to be asked and happy to share advice. Come prepared with specific questions and always follow up with a thank-you note.

Professional Development on a Budget

You don't need expensive conferences or graduate degrees to invest in professional development. Many of the most effective development activities are free or low-cost.

Industry Publications and Podcasts: Stay current with trends in fields you're interested in by reading industry publications (many are free online) and listening to professional podcasts during commutes or workouts.

Volunteer Work: Volunteering for causes you care about can provide professional experience, networking opportunities, and leadership skills. Look for volunteer roles that let you practice skills relevant to your career goals.

Side Projects: Create projects that demonstrate your skills and interests. Build a website, start a blog, create a portfolio, or launch a small business. These projects show initiative and provide concrete examples of your abilities.

Mentorship: Seek out mentors through formal programs at school or work, or by building relationships with professionals you admire. A good mentor can provide career guidance, industry insights, and valuable connections.

Career Planning That Actually Works

Career planning isn't about choosing one job and sticking with it forever – it's about understanding your interests, developing valuable skills, and positioning yourself for opportunities as they arise.

Setting Realistic Career Goals

Short-term Goals (1-2 years): Focus on gaining experience, building skills, and exploring interests. Goals might include completing internships, earning certifications, or building a professional network.

Medium-term Goals (3-5 years): Think about the type of role you want after graduation or in your next career move. What skills, experience, and connections do you need to get there?

Long-term Goals (5+ years): Consider broader career aspirations and lifestyle goals. Do you want to be an expert in a specific field, start your own business, or have a leadership role in an organization?

Financial Reality: The average person changes careers (not just jobs, but entire career fields) several times in their life. So don't stress about picking the "perfect" path right now—just focus on building transferable skills, gaining experience, and learning what excites (and drains) you.

Every job, side hustle, or volunteer gig you take is a step toward clarity. You're not just making money—you're collecting clues about your strengths, values, and direction. Every experience –job or not– will help you get there, so try to get exposed to a myriad of things early on.

Your career isn't something that just "happens" to you. It's something you build—with intention, experimentation, and hustle. Start small, stay curious, and invest in yourself. Over time, that effort compounds into freedom, opportunity, and a life you actually want.

Chapter 8: Financial Goal Setting and Planning

You're scrolling through social media and see your friend posting from their dream vacation in Bali, another friend just bought their first car, and someone else is talking about how they're already saving for a house. Meanwhile, you're sitting there with $47 in your checking account wondering how everyone else seems to have their financial life together.

Here's the truth bomb – they probably don't have it all figured out either, but they might have something you haven't discovered yet: **financial goals**. Not the vague "I want to be rich someday" kind, but actual, specific, achievable goals that turn money dreams into money reality.

The difference between people who build wealth and those who stay broke isn't luck, rich parents, or some secret money hack. It's having a clear plan and working that plan consistently. And the best part? You can start right now, regardless of whether you have $47 or $4,700 in your account.

Financial Reality: According to recent studies, only 34% of young adults have written financial goals, but those who do write them down are 42% more likely to achieve them. That's not coincidence – that's the power of intentional planning.

SMART Financial Goals

Let's start with the foundation. You've probably heard of SMART goals in school or work, but when it comes to money, this framework becomes your financial GPS. It's the difference between saying "I want to save money" and actually having a plan that gets you there.

Specific: Get Crystal Clear About What You Want

Vague goals create vague results. "I want to save money" sounds nice, but it's basically useless. Your brain doesn't know what to do with that information. Instead, get specific about exactly what you're working toward.

Instead of: "I want to save money for college"

Try: "I want to save $5,000 for my sophomore year tuition by August 2025"

Instead of: "I need a car"

Try: "I want to save $3,000 for a reliable used Honda Civic with under 100,000 miles"

Instead of: "I should probably start investing"

Try: "I want to invest $50 per month in a Roth IRA starting this month"

Money Tip: When setting specific goals, include the exact dollar amount, what it's for, and any important details that matter to you. This gives your brain something concrete to work toward.

The more specific you get, the easier it becomes to make daily decisions that support your goal. When you know you need exactly $3,000 for that car, you can figure out that you need to save $250 per month for 12 months. Suddenly, that daily $8 coffee run looks different when you realize it's $240 per month that could go toward your car fund.

Measurable: Track Your Progress Like Your Favorite Game

If you've ever played a video game, you know how satisfying it is to watch your progress bar fill up or see your score increase. Your financial goals need that same kind of tracking system. You need to know exactly where you are and how much further you have to go.

Create milestone markers that let you celebrate small wins along the way. If your goal is to save $2,000 for an emergency fund, set up celebrations at $500, $1,000, and $1,500. These mini-celebrations keep you motivated when the goal feels far away.

Use technology to your advantage. Apps like Mint, YNAB (You Need A Budget), or even a simple spreadsheet can help you track progress. Many banks now offer automatic savings tracking and will send you updates on your progress toward specific goals.

Visual tracking works wonders. Some people love old-school methods like coloring in a thermometer-style chart or using a jar where they can physically see their cash growing. Find what motivates you and use it.

Money Tip: Set up automatic transfers to your goal-specific savings accounts on payday. Even if it's just $25 per paycheck, watching that balance grow automatically feels amazing and keeps you on track without thinking about it.

Achievable: Dream Big, But Plan Realistically

Here's where a lot of people mess up their financial goals – they either aim so low that the goal doesn't motivate them, or they aim so high that they get discouraged and quit. The sweet spot is setting goals that stretch you but don't break you.

Consider your current income and expenses honestly. If you're making $400 per month from your part-time job and your expenses are $350, don't set a goal to save $500 per month. That's setting yourself up for failure and frustration.

Factor in your learning curve. If you've never budgeted before, don't expect to suddenly become a savings machine overnight. Give yourself time to develop good money habits while working toward your goals.

Build in some flexibility. Life happens. Your car might need repairs, or you might have unexpected expenses. Build a small buffer into your timeline so that normal life events don't derail your entire plan.

Start with smaller goals to build confidence. If your ultimate goal is to save $10,000, start with a goal of $1,000. Once you prove to yourself that you can do it, the bigger goals feel more achievable.

Financial Reality: Most financial experts recommend that beginners start by trying to save just 10% of their income. As you get better at managing money and potentially increase your income, you can bump that percentage up.

Relevant: Make Sure Your Goals Actually Matter to YOU

This is huge and often overlooked. Your financial goals need to align with what you actually value and want in life, not what other people think you should want.

Connect your goals to your values. If family is super important to you, maybe your goal is saving for family vacations or building an emergency fund so you can help family members if needed. If adventure is your thing, maybe you're saving for travel or experiences.

Consider your current life stage. A 16-year-old's financial goals should look different from a 24-year-old's goals. Don't feel pressured to have the same priorities as someone in a completely different life situation.

Think about your personal circumstances. If you're planning to go to college, student loan planning might be more relevant than saving for a house down payment right now. If you're already working full-time, retirement savings might be more important than textbook money.

Money Tip: Write down your top 5 life priorities right now. Then look at your financial goals and make sure they support at least one of those priorities. If they don't, either adjust your goals or reconsider your priorities.

Time-bound: Give Yourself Deadlines That Work

Deadlines create urgency and help you stay focused. Without them, financial goals tend to become "someday" dreams that never happen.

Be specific about your timeline. "By next year" is too vague. "By December 31, 2024" gives you something concrete to work with.

Break long-term goals into shorter chunks. If you want to save $6,000 in two years, that's $3,000 per year, $250 per month, or about $58 per week. Suddenly a big scary number becomes much more manageable.

Set both short-term and long-term deadlines. You might have a goal to save $10,000 for college over the next three years, but also set monthly and quarterly check-ins to make sure you're on track.

Account for seasonal variations. If you make more money during summer months, plan for that. If you know you'll have higher expenses during certain times of year (back-to-school, holidays), factor that into your timeline.

Short-term Goals (1 Year)

Short-term goals are your financial foundation. These are the goals that set you up for success with everything else and help you handle the curveballs that life inevitably throws your way.

Emergency Fund: Your Financial Safety Net

Let's start with the most important short-term goal: your emergency fund. I know, I know – "emergency fund" sounds about as exciting as watching paint dry. But hear me out, because this is literally the difference between a minor inconvenience and a major financial disaster.

Start with $1,000. This isn't some random number – it's enough to handle most common emergencies without going into debt. Your phone breaks, your car needs a repair, you have an unexpected medical bill, or you need to help a family member. $1,000 covers most of these situations.

Then work toward 3 months of expenses. Once you have that initial $1,000, start calculating what three months of your essential expenses would cost. If you're living at home, this might be pretty low – maybe just your car payment, insurance, phone bill, and some personal expenses. If you're on your own, include rent, utilities, groceries, and other necessities.

Use a high-yield savings account. Don't just stick this money under your mattress or in a checking account earning nothing. Online banks like Ally, Marcus, or Discover offer savings accounts that earn actual interest. It's not going to make you rich, but why not earn some money while your emergency fund sits there waiting?

Money Tip: Set up automatic transfers to your emergency fund right after payday, before you have a chance to spend the money on other things. Even $25 per paycheck adds up to $650 per year if you get paid bi-weekly.

Keep it separate but accessible. Your emergency fund should be in a different account from your regular spending money, but you should be able to access it quickly when you need it. A savings account works perfectly – separate enough that you won't accidentally spend it, accessible enough that you can get to it in a real emergency.

Debt Payoff: Breaking Free from the Debt Trap

If you have debt – whether it's credit cards, student loans, or money you owe to family – making a plan to pay it off should be one of your top short-term goals. Debt is like a weight dragging down every other financial goal you have.

List all your debts. Write down every single debt you have, including the total amount owed, minimum payment, and interest rate.

Yes, even that $200 you borrowed from your parents. You can't make a plan until you know exactly what you're dealing with.

Choose your payoff strategy. The two most popular methods are:

Debt Snowball: Pay minimums on everything, then throw every extra dollar at the smallest debt first. Once that's paid off, take that payment amount and add it to the next smallest debt.

Debt Avalanche: Pay minimums on everything, then attack the highest interest rate debt first. Mathematically, this saves you the most money.

Find extra money to throw at debt. Look for ways to increase your debt payments beyond the minimums. Pick up extra shifts, sell stuff you don't need, use windfalls like birthday money or tax refunds, or temporarily cut back on non-essential spending.

Financial Reality: The average credit card interest rate is over 20%. That means if you only make minimum payments on a $1,000 credit card balance, you'll pay over $2,000 total and it will take you over 9 years to pay off. Attack that debt aggressively.

Major Purchase: Buying What You Want Without Going Broke

One of the best feelings in the world is buying something you really want with cash you've specifically saved for it. No guilt, no debt, no stress – just pure satisfaction.

Define exactly what you want. If it's a laptop, research the specific model, where you'll buy it, and exactly how much it costs including tax. If it's a car, figure out not just the purchase price but also insurance, registration, and immediate maintenance needs.

Create a dedicated savings account. Many banks let you create multiple savings accounts with specific names. Having a "Laptop Fund" or "Car Fund" makes it feel more real and helps you resist the temptation to spend that money on other things.

Look for ways to reduce the cost. Can you buy it used? Wait for a sale? Use student discounts? Find a promo code? Sometimes a little patience and research can save you hundreds of dollars.

Consider the total cost of ownership. That car isn't just the purchase price – it's also insurance, gas, maintenance, and repairs. That laptop might need software or accessories. Factor in the ongoing costs so you're not surprised later.

Money Tip: Set up a separate savings account for each major purchase goal. Many online banks let you do this for free, and seeing your "Car Fund" grow separately from your "Emergency Fund" helps keep you motivated and organized.

Skill Investment: Betting on Yourself

Some of the best short-term financial goals involve investing in yourself and your future earning potential. These goals might cost money upfront but can pay dividends for years to come.

Professional certifications in your field can lead to promotions or better job opportunities. Research what certifications are valued in your industry and what they cost.

Online courses can teach you valuable skills. Platforms like Coursera, Udemy, or Skillshare offer courses in everything from coding to digital marketing to personal finance.

Professional equipment might be necessary for side hustles or career advancement. A good camera for photography, quality tools for trades, or a reliable computer for remote work.

Networking events and conferences can lead to job opportunities and valuable connections. Yes, they cost money, but they can also open doors that lead to much higher income.

Medium-term Goals (1-5 Years)

Medium-term goals bridge the gap between your immediate needs and your long-term dreams. These goals require more planning and patience, but they're also where you start to see the real power of consistent saving and planning.

Education Funding: Investing in Your Future

Whether you're planning for college, graduate school, or professional development programs, education costs money – often a lot of money.

But the right education can also dramatically increase your earning potential over your lifetime.

Research the real costs. Don't just look at tuition – factor in books, housing, food, transportation, and living expenses. The "sticker price" of college is usually much lower than what you'll actually pay.

Explore all your options. Community college for the first two years, in-state public universities, schools that offer good financial aid, or trade programs that lead directly to good-paying careers. The most expensive option isn't always the best option.

Look into 529 education savings plans. These are special accounts designed for education expenses. The money grows tax-free, and you don't pay taxes when you use it for qualified education expenses.

Don't forget about scholarships and grants. This is free money that you don't have to pay back. Spend time applying for scholarships – it's one of the best "hourly wages" you'll ever earn.

Financial Reality: The average student loan debt for college graduates is over $30,000. Every dollar you can save or earn through scholarships is a dollar you won't have to pay back with interest later.

Career Investment: Building Your Professional Future

Your career is likely to be your biggest source of income for most of your life, so investing in it makes financial sense.

Professional wardrobe might seem shallow, but appearance matters in many careers. You don't need to spend a fortune, but having appropriate clothes for interviews and work can impact your success.

Job training and skill development can lead to promotions, career changes, or side income opportunities. This might be formal education, online courses, or learning from mentors.

Networking and relationship building often requires some investment. This might mean joining professional organizations, attending industry events, or even just having coffee with people in your field.

Professional tools and equipment specific to your career path. This could be anything from quality kitchen knives for a chef to design software for a graphic designer.

Major Purchases: The Big Stuff

Medium-term major purchases are typically things that cost several thousand dollars and significantly impact your life.

Your first car (if you don't have one) or upgrading to a more reliable vehicle. Remember to factor in insurance, maintenance, and repairs when budgeting for a car.

First home down payment might seem impossible, but if homeownership is important to you, it's worth starting to save early.

Even if you're years away from buying, starting the savings habit now makes a huge difference.

Quality investments in things that will last and potentially save you money over time. This might be quality furniture, appliances, or tools that you'll use for many years.

> *Money Tip: For major purchases, create a timeline that works backward from when you want to make the purchase. If you want to buy a $15,000 car in three years, you need to save $5,000 per year, or about $417 per month.*

Relationship Goals: Planning for Two

If you're in a serious relationship or planning to be, some medium-term goals might involve another person.

Wedding savings can help you start your marriage without massive debt. The average wedding costs over $30,000, but you can have a beautiful wedding for much less with planning and creativity.

Joint financial goals with your partner, like saving for a house together or planning a major trip. These goals require communication and compromise.

Family planning costs, if kids are in your future. From pregnancy and birth costs to childcare and everything babies need, kids are expensive. Planning ahead helps.

Long-term Goals (5+ Years)

Long-term goals are where the magic of compound growth really starts to show. These goals might seem far away and abstract now, but starting early – even with small amounts – can make an enormous difference in your financial future.

Retirement Planning

Wait, retirement? Isn't that something people in their 50s and 60s worry about?

Yes... but also no.

Here's the truth: The earlier you start thinking about retirement—even if you're only putting away $20 a month—the easier it becomes to build serious wealth over time. Why? Two words that by now you know very well: **compound interest**.

Retirement Accounts You Should Know About:

- **Roth IRA:** Contribute after-tax money now, and your money grows **tax-free**. When you retire, you pay no taxes on your withdrawals. This is a great option for young people who are in lower tax brackets.

- **Traditional IRA or 401(k):** These reduce your taxable income now, but you'll pay taxes when you withdraw the money in retirement. Often offered by employers with possible matching contributions.

Even if retirement feels decades away, developing the habit of saving—even a tiny amount—helps you lock in a mindset of long-term thinking. It also makes you more likely to hit all your other financial goals in life.

Legacy Goals: Giving and Leaving a Mark

This one's deeper. Once you've stabilized your finances, paid down debts, built savings, and started investing, you might start thinking beyond yourself. What kind of mark do you want to leave on the world?

- **Charitable giving**: Want to support causes you care about? Budgeting for regular giving—or creating a charitable giving fund—can be part of your long-term financial goals.

- **Helping family**: Maybe you want to support younger siblings, aging parents, or future kids. These are big financial goals that require planning.

- **Leaving an inheritance**: This might seem far off, but thinking about what you want your money to do *after* you're gone—whether it's supporting a cause, funding a scholarship, or setting up your family—is part of next-level financial thinking.

A Plan Beats Panic Every Time

Life is unpredictable. Expenses pop up. Plans change. But here's the deal: **a written plan gives you control**.

When you have financial goals that are clear, specific, and aligned with your values, you stop reacting and start making moves with intention. You'll feel more confident, less anxious, and more excited about your future.

You don't have to be rich to start planning. You just have to start. One goal. One step. One good money decision at a time.

Chapter 9: Scams, Fraud & the Money Tricks Your Brain Plays on You

Reality check: a recent FBI Internet Crime Report shows people under 29 lost over **$560 million** to online fraud in just one year, at an average of $7,563 per complaint. Most victims thought "I'd never fall for that." *Spoiler:* we all have blind spots—because scammers know how to hack both **technology** *and* **psychology**.

Why You're a Target

1. **Digital native = bigger footprint.**
   The average 17-year-old has accounts on 8+ platforms. More accounts → more data to steal.

2. **Early credit = clean credit.**
   Your thin credit file is pure gold for identity thieves—they can open loans that go unnoticed longer.

3. **Confidence + curiosity.**
   Gen Z grew up sharing, swiping, and believing rapid-fire content. That same ease lowers the "wait, is this real?" instinct.

The Greatest Hits of Modern Scams

Scam Type	How It Works	Red Flags	Armor-Up Moves
Phishing & Smishing	Fake emails or texts impersonate banks, universities, even friends.	Urgent tone, odd sender address, grammar slips, "verify now" links.	Don't click; open a *new* tab and log in directly. Enable 2-factor authentication (2FA).
Peer-to-Peer Pay-App Hustles	"Oops! Sent $$ to the wrong person—can you refund?" on Zelle/Cash App/PayPal.	Stranger asks you to reverse money; payment marked *completed*.	Treat refunds like sales: only refund *after* original payment clears.
Student-Loan "Relief" Fees	Scammers charge upfront to "fast-track" forgiveness.	Pressure to pay *today*; asks for FAFSA login.	Loan help from studentaid.gov is free. Report fee-for-relief offers.
Crypto & NFT Rug Pulls	Influencer hypes a coin, insiders dump, price collapses.	Promises 5-10× returns "this month," anonymous founders.	Research white paper, lock-up periods, and project Discord history.
Job / Internship Cons	Fake recruiter posts remote gig, then sends you a check to buy equipment—asks for partial refund. The check later bounces.	Gmail address, no interview, "send money back."	Verify company via LinkedIn; insist on direct-deposit *after* your bank clears funds (5–7 days).
Romance & "Sugar" Scams	Online admirer requests gift cards or crypto for a "family emergency."	Never meets in person, love bombs quickly, money talk appears fast.	Video-chat verification before emotional investment. Never wire funds.

Behavioral Biases: Your Brain's Built-In Bugs

Scammers rarely need advanced hacking skills; instead, they hack the wetware between our ears. They understand that every human brain runs on mental shortcuts—"heuristics"—that usually help us make quick decisions but can be weaponized against us. Below are six of the most common traps, explained in plain language with real-life illustrations and a quick defense tactic you can put into practice today.

FOMO — Fear of Missing Out

Your brain loves novelty and hates being left behind. A countdown timer, a flashing "only 17 spots left," or a TikTok influencer screaming that a meme-coin will 10× "by midnight" triggers adrenaline. That cocktail of excitement + anxiety short-circuits rational thought: *What if this is the next Bitcoin and I'm the idiot who skipped it?*

Real-world hit: A Telegram group announces an exclusive crypto presale. You have to send US dollars or Bitcoin within the next hour to secure a "guaranteed allocation." People pile in—only to discover the wallet belongs to the scammer, and the project never existed.

Antidote: institute a **24-hour cool-off rule** for any offer that demands instant payment. Opportunities worth having will still be there tomorrow—or they weren't real opportunities in the first place.

Authority Bias

We're wired to trust uniforms, titles, and blue-check marks. Scammers exploit this reflex by impersonating the IRS, your bank's fraud department, a campus administrator, or a verified celebrity. When an "official" voice tells you to act, you tend to obey before questioning legitimacy.

Real-world hit: You receive an email that looks like it's from "payment@irs.gov" warning that you owe back taxes and must settle *today* via prepaid debit card to avoid arrest. Because it invokes the weight of government authority, victims pay first and verify later—after the money's gone.

Antidote: adopt a **contact-back policy**: hang up or close the message, look up the organization's *public* phone number or website yourself, and initiate the call on your terms.

Scarcity & Urgency

Evolution taught us to grab scarce resources fast—ripe fruit, shelter, social approval. Scammers mimic this pressure with ticking clocks ("sale ends in 10 minutes") or threats ("your Amazon package is on hold"). The artificial deadline makes you focus on *time* instead of *truth*.

Real-world hit: A text claims your online order can't ship until you "confirm payment" within an hour via a link. Victims rush to comply, handing over card credentials to a spoofed site.

Antidote: whenever a message declares **"act now or lose everything,"** flip the script: pause, breathe, and ask, *who benefits if I rush?*

Social Proof

If everyone else is doing it, it *must* be safe—right? That herd instinct helped our ancestors survive but now backfires online. Fraudsters pad Instagram comments with bot endorsements, inflate follower counts, or showcase photoshopped Trustpilot stars to manufacture credibility. Yes, all of this is possible and very easy to do.

Real-world hit: A "fin-fluencer" posts dozens of screenshots showing users who "made $1,200 overnight" with his stock market trading Discord channel or course. In reality, most accounts are fake, and new members finance the scammer's lifestyle through subscription fees.

Antidote: remember that **testimonials can be rented**. Verify claims through independent sources—search the business name + "scam" or "complaint," and check if reviewers have long-standing, real profiles.

Anchoring

The first number you see sets a mental anchor; everything after feels cheap or expensive relative to it, not in absolute terms. Scammers float an absurdly high "normal price" so the "discount" looks irresistible.

Real-world hit: You land on a webinar funnel where a course is "normally $999," slashed to $99 "for the next 50 buyers." You compare $99 to $999 (anchor) instead of asking whether the content is worth $99 at all.

Antidote: ignore the starting sticker and **benchmark against market reality**—look at comparable products or free alternatives before judging value.

Sunk-Cost Fallacy

Once we've invested time or money, our ego pushes us to keep investing so the earlier effort "wasn't wasted." Scammers exploit this by extracting ever-smaller fees to "unlock" a promised payout or recover prior losses.

Real-world hit: After losing $300 to a "VIP crypto mining pool," a victim is told she can retrieve the funds for a $50 "gas fee." She pays, nothing happens, and the scammer requests another $40 to "re-sync the blockchain"—a vicious loop.

Antidote: create a **hard-stop threshold** (e.g., two strikes or $50 lost) after which you walk away, no matter how much pride hurts. Treat additional money as a brand-new decision, not a rescue mission for past spending.

Quick Memory Hook

F-A-S-S-A-S

FOMO · Authority · Scarcity · Social Proof · Anchoring · Sunk-cost

Say it out loud once. The next time you feel that stomach-flip urge to click *"Buy"* or *"Send,"* run the offer through each letter. If it trips one or more, step back and reassess—your wallet will thank you.

Spot-Check: Your 5-Point Fraud Filter

1. **Source** – Do you know and trust the *sender*?

2. **Sense** – Does the message make logical sense? Typos, contradictions?

3. **Pressure** – Is there a rush or threat? Legit orgs rarely demand instant action.

4. **Path** – Where does the link/URL actually lead? Hover to preview.

5. **Payment** – Are they asking for gift cards, crypto, P2P refunds? Giant red flag.

Write "SSPPP" on a sticky note near your laptop for a quick mental pause.

Building an Anti-Scam Toolkit

Layer	Tools & Habits
Digital Hygiene	• Unique passwords via a password manager • 2FA everywhere—authenticator apps beat SMS. • Auto-update OS & antivirus.
Credit Guardrails	• Freeze credit at Experian, Equifax, TransUnion (free, reversible). • Use **virtual card numbers** for online shopping.
Info-Sharing Rules	• Turn off public Venmo feed. • No screenshots of tickets, IDs, or vaccination cards online. • Shred physical mail with barcodes or account info.
Money Movement Mindset	• Treat P2P apps like *cash*: no buyer protection. • For big purchases, use credit cards (built-in fraud dispute rights).
Gut-Check Buddy	• Agree with a friend/parent to sanity-check any request over $100 before sending money. A 30-second call can save $3,000.

Reflection Questions & Micro-Exercises

1. **PhishBowl:** Screenshot the next suspicious email/text you receive (hide personal data) and label the red flags.

2. **Bias Journal:** For one week, note any online ad or post that triggers an emotional urge to buy. Which bias did it tap?

3. **Two-Minute Freeze:** Set a rule: wait 120 seconds before acting on any unexpected money request. How does the pause change your decisions?

Quick-Reference Resources

- **IdentityTheft.gov** – Step-by-step recovery plans (U.S.).

- **haveibeenpwned.com** – Check if your email/password appeared in a breach.

- **ConsumerFinance.gov** – Scam alerts & complaint portal.

- **Stop.Think.Connect tips at http://www.dhs.gov/stopthinkconnect** – Free cyber-safety tip sheets.

Key Takeaways

- Scams succeed when technology + psychology collide.

- Recognize behavioral biases—FOMO, authority, scarcity—to disarm emotional triggers.

- Use a layered defense: strong passwords, credit freeze, "SSPPP" filter, and a gut-check buddy.

- Remember: **If pressure is high and payoff is huge, pause— because real opportunities rarely expire in minutes.**

Chapter 10: Taxes 101. Decode the mystery, keep more money

You open your first pay-stub and—whoa—almost a third of your cash vanished into lines labelled *Fed*, *FICA*, and *State*. Your brain screams, *"What is FICA and why is it robbing me?"*

Taxes feel like a black box until you learn the rules. After that they become another dial you can tweak to reach your money goals faster.

Why taxes exist (and why they're layered)

Most of the "stuff" you rely on every day—streetlights, health inspectors, roads—doesn't pay for itself. Taxes pool money from millions of people so no one has to foot the whole bill when a bridge needs repair or a hurricane hits.

- **Federal income tax** funds the national to-do list: defense, scientific research, student-loan servicing, food-safety labs, you name it.
- **Payroll tax (a.k.a. FICA)** funnels dollars straight into Social Security and Medicare, programs designed to support older Americans.
- **State and local taxes** bankroll teachers, firefighters, and the pothole crew that patches the road to school.

Think of taxes as compulsory membership dues for a functional society—nobody cheers when they pay them, but everyone's glad when our ambulance can make it to the hospital quickly because there is a highway.

The progressive-bracket idea (spoiler: it's fairer than it looks)

Federal Tax Rate	Single Filer	Married Filing Jointly or Surviving Spouse
10%	$0 to $11,925	$0 to $23,850
12%	$11,926 to $48,475	$23,851 to $96,950
22%	$48,476 to $103,350	$96,951 to $206,700
24%	$103,351 to $197,300	$206,701 to $394,600
32%	$197,301 to $250,525	$394,601 to $501,050
35%	$250,526 to $626,350	$501,051 to $751,600
37%	$626,351 or more	$751,601 or more

(July 2025 federal tax brackets - One Big Beautiful Bill Act)

U.S. income tax is progressive: the *next* dollar you earn falls into a higher bracket, but the dollars below keep their lower rates.

Example: If the 12% bracket tops out at $48,475 and you make $48,476, only **one** dollar jumps into the 22% slice. Your *effective* rate (average rate for your entire income) stays much lower than 22%.

Money Tip: When you hear friends say, "I don't want a raise—it'll push me up a bracket," remind them that extra income is never taxed at 100%. The raise still leaves them richer.

Anatomy of a paycheck—where the money goes

A pay-stub feels like alphabet soup, but every line has a job:

Line	Why it's there
Federal Withholding	An estimate of your income-tax bill, forwarded to the IRS each payday.
State Withholding	Same idea, but for your state (if it charges income tax).
FICA	6.2% Social Security + 1.45% Medicare. Your employer quietly matches this amount for a total of 15.3%. This means that the cost the company pays for having you as an employee is larger than just your salary.
Pre-tax deductions	401(k) deposits, Health Savings Account (HSA) contributions, or transit passes—money that skips the tax calculation for now.

Result: You may earn $600 in gross pay but see only $390 land in checking. The disappearing dollars didn't evaporate; they went to future-you (retirement), grandma (Social Security), and community-you (roads, schools).

Withholding is just a forecast

Your employer guesses your yearly tax via the **W-4** form you filled out. Life changes—raises, side hustles, moving states—can make that guess too high (you'd get a big refund) or too low (you'd have to pay extra when taxes are filed in April). Aim for a Goldilocks middle ground:

- **Refund under $100:** you didn't loan the government a lot of free money with each paycheck.
- **Bill under $100:** easy to pay without tapping into savings.

Adjusting is easy: revisit the IRS Withholding Estimator online, then hand HR an updated W-4.

Filing a return—your annual report card

Between January and April 15th, you pull together W-2s (wages), 1099s (side income), and perhaps a 1098-T (tuition paid). You shuffle the numbers onto **Form 1040** using:

1. **IRS Free File** – for incomes under $84,000.
2. **VITA** sites – volunteer tax pros on many campuses.
3. **Tax software** – TurboTax, H&R Block for user-friendly software that helps you along the way.

File early—identity thieves love beating you to the punch.

Credits > Deductions—learn the superstar perks

- **Standard deduction**: the IRS provides a generous standard deduction—a set amount of income that is automatically shielded from tax, which simplifies filing for most young people. This amount is adjusted for inflation each year. It was about $15,800 for single filers in 2025.
- **Itemizing** makes sense only when mortgage interest, charity, and state taxes beat that standard deduction.

Credits slice the bill dollar-for-dollar:

- **Child Tax Credit** – up to $2,000 for each child under 17
- **American Opportunity Credit** – up to $2,500 per year for undergrad tuition and books.
- **Saver's Credit** – up to $1,000 for single filers that rewards low-to-mid-income workers for stashing money in a 401(k) or IRA.
- **Lifetime Learning Credit** – 20% off tuition for grad school or professional certificates.

Fast fact: A $1,000 credit is worth roughly eight times more than a $1,000 deduction if you're in the 12% bracket.

Side-hustle reality (self-employment tax 101)

No boss means no automatic withholding. You are now both employee *and* employer:

- You owe the full 15.3% FICA, though you later deduct half as a business expense.
- The IRS expects **quarterly payments**. Mark the 15th of April, June, September, and January.
- Every legit expense—mileage, editing software, part of your phone bill—shrinks your taxable profit, so keep those receipts in a cloud folder.

Refund envy vs. wealth building

A four-figure refund can feel like a bonus, but it's really a pay-stub correction. Imagine having that money drip into a high-yield savings account or a Roth IRA all year instead:

- $150 per month at 5% APY *(example rate, Jan 2025)* = $1,843 after one year, which is more than a $1,800 refund sitting interest-free with Uncle Sam.
- Small tweaks today compound for decades; your tax strategy and your investment strategy must go hand in hand.

Level-up moves for future-you

Tool	Why it's powerful
Roth IRA	Pay tax now, enjoy tax-free growth forever. Great if you're in a low bracket today.
HSA	Triple threat: tax-free going in, tax-free while it grows, tax-free coming out for medical bills.
529 Plan	Tax-free growth for education expenses—yours or a future kid's. Some states also offer upfront deductions.

Keep the IRS happy—record keeping in two clicks

1. Create a cloud folder named **Taxes 2025**.
2. Drop PDFs of every W-2, 1099, tuition bill, donation receipt, and business expense spreadsheet.
3. Keep personal returns **three years** and self-employment docs **five years**—the audit window.

With digital storage you never dig through shoeboxes come audit time.

Quick recap

- Taxes fund the common good and use a bracket system, so only *extra* dollars get higher rates.
- Your pay-stub deductions are *estimates*—adjust them so April isn't a financial roller-coaster.
- Deductions trim taxable income; **credits** annihilate the bill—learn the ones that fit your stage of life.
- Side gigs require quarterly self-employment payments, but deducting real expenses softens the blow.
- Optimizing taxes isn't greed—it's efficiency. Every dollar you *keep* can grow, compound, and fund the life you actually want.

Master these basics now, and tax season transforms from "Ugh, paperwork" to a routine check-in on a wealth-building machine you control.

Final Thoughts: Your Money, Your Future

Let's be real—personal finance can feel overwhelming. Between budgeting apps, investing acronyms, credit scores, and a million hot takes on social media, it's easy to wonder: *"Am I doing this right?"*

If you made it to this point in the book, here's the answer: **Yes. You're doing the right thing by learning, asking questions, and taking control of your future.**

You don't need to be perfect with money. You just need to be *intentional*. The truth is, most people float through life making random money decisions and hoping it all works out. But not you. You've now seen how budgeting, saving, investing, managing debt, and setting goals actually *fit together*. You have a system—a map.

Here's What Really Matters

- **Spend less than you earn.** Simple but powerful.

- **Save consistently.** Even small amounts create massive results over time.

- **Invest early and often.** Compound growth is your secret weapon.

- **Avoid high-interest debt.** It's modern slavery and steals your future freedom.

- **Know your why.** Money is just a tool—make sure you're using it to build a life that excites you.

What's Next?

You don't need to master everything overnight. The most important thing is to **start small and stay consistent**. Pick one habit—whether that's checking your bank account weekly, saving $10 from every paycheck, or opening your first Roth IRA—and commit to it. Then build from there.

As your income grows, your expenses will try to keep up. Fight that urge. Grow your savings, grow your investments, grow your options.

You Are Not Too Young

You're not too young to invest.
You're not too young to start a business.
You're not too young to make smart financial decisions.

The earlier you start, the more freedom, confidence, and opportunity you'll create for yourself down the road.

Final Encouragement

You won't get everything right. Nobody does. But every step you take toward financial awareness is a step toward freedom. Toward peace of mind. Toward saying "yes" to the things that matter and "no" to the things that don't.

Personal finance isn't just about dollars and cents. It's about building the life you want—on purpose.

You've got this. Go build something amazing.

MAP IT OUT
LEARNING GUIDES

Thank you!

Please review us on amazon

★★★★★

Visit **MapItOutBooks.com**
For More Learning Guides

Glossary

529 Plan – A special account that lets your money grow tax-free when it's used for qualified education costs—tuition, books, even some housing. Many states also give an upfront tax break on contributions.

APY (Annual Percentage Yield) – The real return you earn on savings once compounding is factored in. Always compare APY, not just the "interest rate," when shopping bank accounts.

Compound Interest – "Earning interest on interest." Your balance snowballs because each new dollar of earnings itself starts earning. Starting early makes the snowball massive.

Credit Score – A three-digit number (300-850) that acts like your financial GPA. Lenders use it to judge how reliably you pay back debt.

Credit Utilization – The slice of your available credit you're using right now. Keeping it below 30%—ideally under 10%—protects your credit score.

Emergency Fund – Cash set aside for true surprises—job loss, medical bills, car breakdowns. Start with $500–$1,000 and build toward three months of essential expenses.

ETF (Exchange-Traded Fund) – A basket of stocks or bonds you buy like a single stock. Offers instant diversification and usually lower fees than mutual funds.

FDIC Insurance – Federal protection that guarantees up to $250,000 per depositor if a U.S. bank fails.

FICA – The payroll tax that funds Social Security and Medicare: 6.2% + 1.45%, matched by employers. Shows up as a separate line on every pay-stub.

High-Yield Savings Account – An online savings account paying far more interest (often 4%-5% APY) than a traditional brick-and-mortar bank. Ideal parking spot for your emergency fund.

HSA (Health Savings Account) – Triple tax perk: money goes in pre-tax, grows tax-free, and comes out tax-free for medical expenses.

Index Fund – A mutual fund or ETF designed to mimic a market benchmark (e.g., the S&P 500). Low-cost, "set-it-and-forget-it" investing.

Overdraft Fee – The $35 (or more) a bank charges when it covers a purchase after your checking balance hits zero. Opting out of overdraft protection avoids the fee—your card just declines.

Roth IRA – A retirement account where you pay tax now so all future growth and withdrawals after age 59½ are tax-free. Powerful when you're in a low tax bracket today.

Self-Employment Tax – The full 15.3% FICA bill solo entrepreneurs pay on net profit (you're both employee and employer). Quarterly payments keep you out of trouble.

Standard Deduction – A fixed dollar amount the IRS lets you subtract from income before computing tax. Makes filing simple for most young adults.

Tax Credit – A direct dollar-for-dollar cut in your tax bill. Education credits (American Opportunity, Lifetime Learning) or the Saver's Credit can be worth hundreds—or thousands—back in your pocket.

W-2 – The form your employer sends each January summarizing wages earned and taxes withheld; you use it to file your return.

W-4 – The form you give HR to tell them how much tax to withhold from each paycheck. Update it after raises, or moving states.

Withholding – The pay-as-you-earn system where your employer sends estimated income tax to the IRS each payday; you reconcile the total when you file in April.